History of Education
A Study

History of Education

A Study

M. Anjanappa

ANMOL PUBLICATIONS PVT. LTD.
NEW DELHI - 110 002 (INDIA)

ANMOL PUBLICATIONS PVT. LTD.
H.O.: 4374/4B, Ansari Road, Daryaganj
New Delhi - 110 002
Ph.: 23261597, 23278000
B.O.: No. 1015, Ist Main Road, BSK III Stage
III Phase, III Block
Bangalore - 560 085 (India)
Visit us at: www.anmolpublications.com

History of Education: A Study

First Published, 2006

ISBN 81-261-2616-7

PRINTED IN INDIA

Published by J.L. Kumar for Anmol Publications Pvt. Ltd., New Delhi - 110 002 and Printed at Mehra Offset Press, Delhi.

Dedicated to
My Guru
Late Dr. R Ramakrishnan
Lecturer
Department of History
Bangalore University
Bangalore 560056

Contents

Foreword ix

Preface xi

List of Tables xii

1. Introduction 1

2 Growth of Primary Education in Mysore Princely State 11

3. Growth of Secondary Education in Mysore Princely State 34

4. Educational Policy and Legislation 45

5. Educational Administration and Controlling Agencies in Mysore Princely State 76

6. Financing of Education in Mysore Princely State 90

7. Major Findings of the Study 97

Bibliography 110

Index 118

Foreword

I am extremely happy to know the Book **History of Education: A Study** authored by Dr. M. Anjanappa, the benefits of which are useful for both **students of 'History'** and **students of 'Education'.** History is said to be an unending dialogue between present and the past. As such any amount of creation of literature on History is not only significant but also an intensive revision of what had been written already. This cycle of writing and re-writing keeps the History alive. During the last few years there have been lot of changes in the concept of History which has motivated many historians to re-think the subject. Some of the areas of human knowledge are most affected by these changes especially intellectual and cultural history. Various factors contribute to the growth of human culture. Development of human culture itself is historic in nature. To identify these contributing factors from time to time becomes the process of revision of historical records and research the 'Lost' one. What was not found in earlier works would be present in the subsequent efforts. Such is the process of searching for the truth. Historians are now committed to this noble task.

Education plays an important role in promoting growth and development of human resources which in turn accelerate economic development of the nation. The Government of India has also substantially increased the investment in education from pre-primary to tertiary education considering educational process as a holistic process. Now everywhere the focus is on type of system which is termed as accountability linked to school performance. When these factors become prominent in education, there is a need to know the historical background on which the present education is emerged. Swami Vivekananda said that "Education is Manifestation of the Perfection already Present in Man." Man has been changing by contributing his best to the society. Man is no more the Static Stigma of the globe. When every thing is changing, decisions regarding the type of education suitable to the time are to be made systematically. To check this state of affair, landmarks in the History of Indian Education help in a long way. Based on our previous experience and gains, the future of education could be shaped. The new educational experiments have been helping to solve the riddles of the period. It is in this context, the present book serves as a mirror to see our ups and downs in the way of education.

I wish Dr. M. Anjanappa to continue his best efforts in such creative activities.

Dr. M.S. Thimmappa
Vice-Chancellor,
Bangalore University, Bangalore

Preface

The book History of Education: A Study is a sincere effort of mine to present the ideas in a simple way. The main aim is to make the readers friendly and easy to digest the information.

A number of people have been helpful to me in writing this book. I acknowledge those well wishers who inspired me to write this book and thank them for their suggestions.

I am deeply beholden to Dr. M.S. Thimmappa, Hon'ble Vice-Chancellor, Bangalore University, for writing the foreword to this book. I thank Dr. O. Anantharamaiah, Hon'ble Vice-Chancellor, Tumkur University, Tumkur and Dr. M.S. Talawar, Prof. of Education, Bangalore University, Bangalore for their timely help in preparing this book. I also thank T.A. Mohan and Shivashankar. I am thankful to my wife Smt. Seethalakshmi and my daughters Spurthi and Neha for their cooperation. I also thank Mr. J.L. Kumar, Managing Director, Anmol Publications Pvt. Ltd. and Shri V. Srinivasamurthy, Resident Sales Executive (South), Anmol Publications Pvt. Ltd, New Delhi for their generous help to bring out this book at the earliest possible.

Dr. M. Anjanappa

List of Tables

1.	No. of Schools, Teachers and Students	15
2.	District wise Schools	16
3.	District and Hobli Schools	17
4.	Showing peoples in Hobli Schools by Religion/Caste	18
5.	Enrollment of Children	20
6.	Establishment of Schools	20
7.	Total No of Pupils	22
8.	Grant-in-aid Schools	23
9.	Compulsory Primary Education	27
10.	Fresh Schools started	28
11.	Schools under private Management	29
12.	Dropping out of Students from the Schools	29
13.	Dropping out of Students in first year Primary Education	30
14.	Schools Transferred to Local Bodies	31
15.	Enrollment of Boys and Girls	32
16.	Interior Anglo-Vernacular Schools	35
17.	Vernacular Schools 1871-1872	36
18.	Position of Taluk Vernacular Schools 1873-74	38
19.	Growth of Schools in Mysore	39

20. Type of Schools and Enrollment of Students 43

21. No. of Boys and Girls in High Schools 44

22. No. of Caste wise break up of Pupils in High Schools 44

23. No. of Pupils studying in the English Lower Secondary and Higher Classes in the State 60

24. Statement of Hostels attached to Institutions in the State 62

25. Statement of Hostels attached to Institutions in the State 64

26. Statement Showing Freeships Granted to Different Communities 66

27. Statement Showing no. Scholarships Granted to Different Communities 67

28. Statement of Appointment Held by the Different Communities in the State Service 68

29. Statement of Employees in the Government Service Compared with Total Population and the Literature Among them 70

30. Panchayats in the Hobli Schools 79

31. No. of Visits 84

32. No. of Visits 85

33. Expenditure towards Education 91

34. Financial allocation for Education 92

35. Percentage of Expenditure on Service Heads 94

36. Growth of Financial allocation to Education 96

1

Introduction

Historiography

British rule in India was both direct and indirect. While British India was under the direct administration of the imperial power, there were numerous princely states which were indirectly controlled by the paramount power. These princely states also described as Indian-India. The native states consisted of more than 600 big and small princely states. Any comprehensive study of British rule in India will obviously have to take into account these states and British indirect rule therein. In fact, the dynamics of British rule can be clearly understood only when British rule in these states is also studied.

But, till about the early 1960's historiographic activity in respect of modern India was lopsided. The historian generally concentrated on British rule in British India and ignored the princely states. There were reasons for this situation. When, in the nineteenth century the English East India Company came out with the very clever subsidiary alliance system and later Doctrine of Lapse, they also advanced the politically motivated view that the administration of the princely states was marked by gross corruption and that misadministration was the routine. This political view got carried over to historiography and the historian of modern India generally closed his eyes to the princely states. Secondly, and equally significant the Marxist view that the princely states were all anti-people in every thing and always, also added strength to the lopsided historiographic overview.

In 1960 addressing the modern Indian section of the Indian History congress, S.P. Sen exhorted historians to urgently study the history of these princely states. Practically as if responding to this call princely states got into the historiographic agenda after 1960.

Among the princely states, Mysore occupied an important place. Firstly, Mysore was among the states, second largest in territorial extent. Secondly, from the closing years of the 19th Century, Mysore acquired the appellation of Model State. Thirdly, after 1881 the state came to be administered by a set of brilliant personalities as Dewans. One may extend the list and advance many more reasons for Mysore being considered as an important princely states in British Indian records and the contemporary public press.

As on date, there are very few scholarly studies published dealing with the history of Mysore. Historiography of Mysore may be said to begin with C. Hayavadana Rao's *Mysore Gazetteer* published between 1929 and 1932. This work obviously from its title was limited in scope in so far as it was a gazetteer compiling all important facts and a mass of important data. It was published by the Government of the Mysore Maharaja which owed allegiance to the Paramount Power and its author naturally could not critically analyse the details of developments in any field.

Closely following Hayavadana Rao, M. Shama Rao, one time Inspector General of Education of Mysore, published two volumes titled *Modern Mysore* in 1936. This work is dedicated to the Maharaja of Mysore. While in many ways Shama Rao goes beyond a mere compilation of information and to a very limited extent analyses the data he too is far from critical in his approach.

These apart three full length studies on the history of Mysore, have appeared till now. The first of these in point of time is by James Manor. The author is a political scientist and he has discussed the political changes in the state between 1917 and 1956. Next we have B. Hettne's study of the political and economic developments in Mysore in the context of indirect rule. Lastly S. Chandrashekar's study of the dimensions of social and political changes in Mysore between 1918 and 1940 all these authors have concentrated on political and economic changes basically. Chandrashekar is the only exception in a limited way in so far as he discusses some of the development in the field, of education in Mysore also.

In 1985, under the sponsorship of the government of Mysore two senior officials of the education department of Mysore brought out a work titled *History of Education in Mysore*. This work while dealing with the history of education more comprehensively than Hayavadana Rao and Shama Rao like the earlier works lacks critical analysis.

Thus even the Historiographic activity in respect of Mysore is lopsided. The concentration has been on political and economic activities almost entirely. Such a trust is one of the obvious results of colonialism. For the political and economic impact of colonialism are glaring and naturally in the period when India is no more a colony, these aspects are avidly studied. As a matter of fact the same statement to a limited extent may be made with regard to modern India's historiography generally also.

British colonialism had a cultural and intellectual agenda also. Infact the cultural and intellectual impact of colonialism have had serious consequences. Today historians seriously question the facile view of the entirely positive impact of colonialism on Indian intellect and culture. Culturally and intellectually also India was colonized and policies and programmes were developed by the imperial power to keep India subservient in these spheres also and Education obviously forms, an important aspect of intellectual and cultural history.

Aims

This study covers the period between 1854 and 1940. In 1854 the Halifax dispatch which sketched the plan for educational development in India was applied to Mysore State. Prior to this, to quote the words of sir Mark Cubbon " It must be admitted that the administration of Mysore makes no particular show under the head of Education. In an abstract point of view this is to be regretted, but subject nations are not kept in order and Good humour on abstract principles and it has long been the opinion of some, and is rapidly becoming the opinion of many, that the efforts which have been made by government to extend the blessings of education by tests and examination to secure the services of enlightened men even in the lowest posts are not calculated to be so fully appreciated as they ought, by any class of the "Community". While several aspects of this statement are questionable, it indicates 1854 as a convenient benchmark for study. In 1940, the Government of Mysore withdrew the Elementary Education Act which was introduced in 1930.

During the first fifty years after British Colonial penetration, had begun the state authority did nothing regarding education. But an educational system did exist in Mysore which though not modern was useful in its own way. Gradually after 1831, as part of the instructions of the Governor General that the natives should be appointed in the lower rungs of the bureaucracy some attempts were made to establish schools of a elementary nature. Parallelly, Christian Missionary organizations also begun efforts in the educational field for their own purposes. But, it was only after 1857 when the Department of Public Instruction was established that systematic activity began. First the Devereux Scheme, later, the Hobli School Scheme aimed at establishing and expanding primary education which was defined as first four year of schooling. In 1907 the Hobli School scheme was given up. The next stage in Primary education begins with the Dewanship of Visveswaraya which ran parallely with the backward classes movement. Later in 1921 the Government passed orders on the first clear policy document on education namely the education memorandum. From here till 1831 is the next Stage. In 1931 the Mysore Elementary Education Regulation was brought into force and it was in effect till 1941. These developments are discussed in Chapter 2.

The third Chapter discusses middle school education and secondary school education till 1941. Middle Schools which instructed pupils for 4 years after the Primary stage were part of the Primary stage till 1921 though were distinct and had to be separated. Secondary education iminated with the SSLC examination. The developments in these two stages were crucial for two reasons. First, Government jobs required a pass atleast in the Middle School final examination and for certain posts the SSLC was minimum.

Educational policy and statutes form the subject or the next chapter. Here a discussion of the schemes mentioned above and the statutes for education passed in 1913 and 1931 are discussed in detail. The next chapter 5 discusses the controlling agencies and inspectorate over the years till 1941. Here a discussion is undertaken not so much from the point of view of administrative or bureaucratic details though information on this is provided. Rather, the chapter discusses the changing face of the controlling agencies over the years.

Educational activity in the modern period by and large depends upon finance by the state authority. The next chapter

(Chapter 6) discusses the nature and implications of educational finance in Mysore State till 1941 the last chapter (Chapter 7) brings out the findings.

Limitations of the Study

The present study does not aim to be a comprehensive account of the development of education in Mysore. It proposes to deal only with Primary and secondary education and finances and controlling agencies of the educational system at these levels. It does not deal with such aspects as women's education., Muslim education the education and training of teachers at primary and secondary levels or the history of normal schools, education Panchamas and other aspects. Further at the primary and Secondary levels also the study shall make only incidental references to the subjects taught as it requires a distinct work beyond the scope of this work. Further this study shall only refer incidentally to the grant-in-aid system. Since comprehensive discussion of this aspect is also beyond the scope of this work.

British Policy and Mysore

As already noted between 1799 and 1947 Mysore was a Subsidiary ally of the British. During this period, three different engagements were concluded between the Paramount Power and Mysore, namely in 1799, 1881, 1913. All these three engagement broadly defined the extent of power and authority wielded by the princely state. They indicated the functional latitude that was given by the paramount power to the state. Further according to all the princely state had to all times closely conform to the advice of the Paramount Power. Naturally the princely authorities never initiated any distinct development scheme because of the possibility of the scheme being rejected by the Paramount power. All legislature enactments had to receive the prior sanction of the paramount power. The results was that the princely authority usually followed the lines of statutes, and developments initiated by the paramount power in British India after some time.

Critical Directions

The present study is not set within any theoretical framework. However, the study shall seek to examine the extent of validity of the Model State appellation given to Mysore in official and public discussion in British India during the late 19th and 20th centuries. The Model State tag has been applied to Mysore in the context of various developments such as the founding of the Representative Assembly, Legislative Council industrial development and so on. But in recent years studies of various aspects of the history of Mysore in the years after 1881 have led to doubts about the validity of the Model State tag. Further, regarding the development of education in modern India there are generally two views. The first views is that there was in India at the time when English education was introduced a very fine system of education which would bear comparison with the education system which existed then in England It is also held that the British gradually killed this wonderful native or indigenous education system and replaced a modern system and this latter was not useful for the country. This view was expressed by nationalists generally. The second view was that the argument of a fine native educational system was just a myth. This view was expressed by hardcore British administrators usually. While the present study does not entirely validate either of these views, it critically points towards the former, the nationalists view of modern education of India.

Sketch of the History of Mysore 1800-1940

Although from the point of view of the development of education in Mysore, the year 1857, when the Mysore Education Department was formed would be a convenient starting point to comprehend education within the frame work of British colonialism and its influences in the state, it is necessary to go back to the year 1800. It was in 1799 after the IV Mysore war that the State came under colonial influences.

In 1799 Tippu Sultan was defeated by the armies of the English East India company in the IV Mysore War. Subsequently his Kingdom was portioned and one part was renamed Mysore. This State was granted to the Wodeyar representative Krishnaraja Wodeyar as a Subsidiary State.

Since in 1799 Krishnaraja Wodeyar III was a minor Dewan Purnaiah was given the responsibility of administering the state. Purnaiah reorganized the administrative system of Mysore and functioned as Dewan till 1812 under the guidance of British Residents. That year, differences arose between the Prince and the Dewan which finally resulted in the retirement of latter. Purnaiah died shortly afterwards.

After the retirement of Dewan Purnaiah, Krishnaraja Wodeyar III administered the state independently for some time and with the assistance of Dewans for some time. In the year 1831 a peasant uprising took place in the province of Nagar in the Shimoga district of Mysore State. With the assistance of the armies of the East India Company the revolt was put down.

A Committee was constituted to enquire into the causes of the 1831 revolt and this Committee in its report put the entire blame on the ruler Krishnaraja Wodeyar III and charged him with maladministration. Hence citing the conditions of the Subsidiary Treaty the Company took over the administration of Mysore and set aside Krishnaraja Wodeyar III.

Between 1831 and 1881 for exactly 50 years, Mysore came under direct British influence. Between 1831 and 1862 Mark

Cubbon was the Commissioner of the state and he was succeeded by L.B. Bowring (1862-70), and Richard Meade, R.A. Dalyell, C.B. Saunders and James Gordon between 1870-1881.

During the 50 years of direct British rule not only was the administration of the state completely reorganized on colonial lines, the state witnessed the penetration of Christian missionaries on a large scale, Western culture entered Mysore. It was a part of this process that in 1857, the Education Department was formed and the history of modern education in Mysore State begins.

In 1881 as a result of a variety of circumstances and causes the state was restored to the native rule under the terms of the Instrument of Transfer of that year. After the restoration of native rule in 1881 the Mysore Representative Assembly was founded during the Dewanship of C. Rangacharlu, Krishnaraju wodeyar had passed away even before 1881 and he was succeeded by Chamarajendra Wodeyar X.

Charamarjendra Wodeyar X ruled Mysore till 1902 and after his death that year Krishnaraja Wodeyar IV became the Maharaja of Mysore. In 1940 after the death of Krishnaraja Wodeyar IV Jayachamaraja Wodeyar became the ruler of the state.

Between 1881 and 1940 the following persons were the Dewans of Mysore.

1.	C.V. Rangacharlu	1881-1882
2.	K. Seshadri Iyer	1883-1901
3.	P.N. Krishnamurthy	1901-1906
4.	V.P. Madhava Rao	1906-1909
5.	T. Ananda Rao	1909-1912
6.	M. Visweswaraya	1912-1918

7.	M. Kantharaje Urs	1918-1922
8.	A.R. Bannerji	1922-1926
9.	Mirza M. Ismail	1926-1941

In 1907, the Mysore Legislative Council was founded. In 1913 during the Dewanship of M. Visweswaraya, some of the harsh terms of the 1881 engagement were removed and the new Mysore Treaty was signed between the Paramount Power and the Princely state. Further the state witnessed several significant developments, after 1911. Firstly, that very year the Mysore Economic Conference was founded to systematically direct the all round development of the state. In 1912 the backward classes movement demanding preferential treatment for the backward classes began. In 1919 the state issued the first policy document on education, the Education Memorandum under the guidance of C.R. Reddy the then Inspector General of Education of the state. In 1918 the state Government appointed the Leslie C. Miller committee to devise ways and means of improving the position of backward classes in the state in government jobs and education. In 1921 the state Government issued orders on the recommendations of the Miller Committee. In 1924 the state constitution was given a statutory basis following the recommendations of the B.N. Seal Committee for constitutional reforms. In 1930-31 the state brought into effect the Compulsory Elementary Education statute a landmark in the history of education in Mysore state. After a 10 years long experiment this statute was withdrawn in 1940, the year when the present study closes.

2

Growth of Primary Education in Mysore Princely State

State of Education Between 1800-1854

In 1813 a very important debate took place in the House of Commons relating to the religious and moral instruction in India. In this debate Thomas Munro gave evidence regarding the state of school education in the Madras Presidency wherein he said that every village in the presidency had a school. Following this debate the Company Government instructed its officials in India to collect information regarding indigenous schools. Accordingly the Assistant Collector of Srirangapatnam reported to the Board of Revenue of Madras wherein he said that there were 41 schools in Srirangapatnam where "nothing more is professed to be taught than reading writing and arithmetic just competent for the discharge of the common daily transactions of society". Further the Assistant Collector noted that there were 627 pupils in these schools of which 613 were males of these 7.8% were Brahmins, 3.75% Vysyas, 48.61% were Sudras, 25.77% were other communities and 14.62% were Muslims. Significantly all the 14 female pupils were Sudras by caste.

This report indicates several important points. Firstly, the British did not consider the indigenous education as education at all. Secondly though indirectly, it indicates the aims of education as conceived by the British. Thirdly, these comments indicate that the Colonial power thought education had to be sponsored and supported by the State.

While the 1822 Report thought very poorly of the native education system in Mysore, it was not till 1857 that the Government initiated steps for the development of what was considered as systematic activity in education. But between 1800 and 1854, desultory activity did take place by way of starting schools. And in starting these modern schools (to distinguish these institutions from the indigenous educational institutions) the first steps were taken by Christian Missionaries especially those of the London Christian Mission and the Wesleyan Mission. The first such school was started by the London Mission in 1827 in Bangalore and in 1840 a Kannada Day School for girls in the same place. Earlier in 1833, under encouragement from the British Resident General Fraser the. Maharaja Krishnaraja wodeyar III started a school for teaching English in Mysore called the Rajah's School.

A very limited number of children (boys) went to this institution and in 1840 the Maharaja placed the school under the Wesleyan Mission. It continued thus till 1850 and later came back to the ruler's control. This school had a chequered career. Till 1857 the following schools were started in the state.

1. Ordanance School, Fort, Bangalore -1832
2. Raja's High School, Mysore -1833
3. Wesleyan Mission School, Gubbi -1840
4. Madrasa Ebrahim, Echinapalli -1840
5. Wesleyan Muission School, Fort gate, Tumkur -1842
6. Sadar Vedasiddantha Sabha School, Bangalore -1842
7. London Mission Boarding Home for Girls, Bangalore -1842
8. Wesleyan Mission School, Hosahalli -1843
9. St.Paul's Mission School, Bangalore -1945

10. London Mission Institution, Bangalore -1847
11. Native Educational Institution, Bangalore -1851
12. Wesleyan Mission School, Hassan -1852
13. Wesleyan Mission School, Tumkur -1852
14. Wesleyan Mission School, Shimoga -1854
15. London Mission Contonment School, Bangalore -1854
16. St.Mark's Catholic School, Bangalore -1854
17. St.Mark's Regged School, Bangalore -1854
18. St.John's District School for Girls, Bangalore -1854
19. St.John's English Infant School for Girls, Bangalore -1854
20. Hindu Female School, Bangalore -1854
21. Wesleyan Mission School, Mysore -1854
22. Wesleyan Mission Day School (Girls), Mysore -1855
23. London Mission Girls School, Cubbonpet, Bangalore -1856
24. Madrasa Islamia, Chintamani -1856
25. St.John's District School, Bangalore -1856

Several points need to be noted regarding these early institutions. Firstly, most of these were started by Christian Missions. Secondly, in these schools started by Christian Missions a large part of the instruction was in the Bible and religious subjects. Thirdly, these schools did not attract all the sections of Mysore society and lastly most of them had a chequered career. It is also important that all of there were private schools and the Government was still far away from educational activity.

Devereux Scheme

In 1855 the Government of Mysore sent to the government of India the first proposal for development of education in the state. This note to the school Commission of the Government of India observed that, "in a country where nothing really is considered a prize, the obtaining of sirkar employment through a certificate from educational authorities may induce people to take to education". While this objective was "Inferior" and education should aim at elevating the character of the community and individual, this proposal suggested that English schools be started in the principal towns with teachers being paid respectable salaries and given free houses. Pupils were to pay a fee of 4 Ana's per month nothing came out of this proposal for, the next year, under the woods, dispatch as applied to Mysore a scheme for the development of education was approved by the Government of India.

According to the Devereux scheme, there were to be Anglo Vernacular Schools one in each Division, 80 Vernacular Schools, one in each taluk and 2 Normal schools one each for the Malnad and Maidan areas of the State. These were to be under a Central College. Fees were to be charged in all schools to make people understand that they, and not the Government would benefit from education. Further, taluk schools were to be established only when the people residing in that area applied for it. The full complement of these schools were to be established over several years.

Under this scheme the schools that already existed in Hassan, Tumkur and Shimoga and the Raja's School at Mysore were taken over as Divisional Anglo-Vernacular Schools. The Native Educational Institution at Bangalore took the place of the Central College. All other schools continued.

While schools at the taluk level were to be established on application from the people, if in any taluk applications were not forthcoming Government was to start schools, on an experimental basis. If even this did not attract popular attention, a notice was to be published that persons who could not read and write their Vernacular would not be eligible for Government employment in the salary level of the Rs.6 and above per month.

Application from residents in many taluks came and

schools were started in taluks. Available dates regarding these schools is presented in Table 1.

TABLE 1

No. of Schools, Teachers and Students

	Government		*Aided*		*Total*	
	Schools	*Pupils*	*Schools*	*Pupil*	*School*	*Pupil*
1859-1860	N.A.	622	N.A.	385	N.A.	1,007
1860-1861	N.A.	1,162	5	499	N.A.	1,661
1861-1862	8	616	5	642	13	1,258
1862-1863	13	990	14	1,383	27	2,373

This Table indicates (1) contrary to the expressions of the Government this scheme was generally not popular for, there were many taluks which did not apply for schools. (2) Among the schools started, the Government schools were not as popular, as the aided schools. Thus Cubbons remarks in 1860, to the foreign department that there was "Comparatively title anxiety" for education in Mysore is clear. Earlier in 1857 he had made similar observation and concluded that even the bait of employment in the lowest ranges of governmental ladder were not taken by the people of Mysore.

Hobli School Scheme (1868-1900)

Following on the observation by the Government of India regarding absence of schools specially for female children and the need to increase Vernacular schools in Mysore. B.L. Rice drew up the Hobli school Scheme in 1868. This was approved by the Foreign Department the same year.

Under this scheme one school was to be started in every Hobli in the state so that no village was more then 4 1/2 miles away from a school. These hobli schools were to be open both for boys and girls. Each school was to have a

Panchayat consisting of leading citizens of the place to supervise the work of the institutions. Notifications detailing the scheme were widely publicised and it seems that it was welcomed by the people. Below we give a sample of a petition from people for starting such school from the report of the year 1868-69. We who are the residents of the following 13 villages situated in the Hobli of the — Taluk desire to express the great joy (Maha santhosha) with which we have all received the Istihar stating that Government will establish schools in every Hobli for the education of all classes. Had the khavind issued such on order before what great blessings should we already have enjoyed. Even now as the khavind has conferred such favour upon us, and no matter could be of greater importance, we undertake to build a house near to and in the middle of, these 13 villages, and earnestly pray that Government will appoint a Canarese master to instruct our 79 children.

Gives the Details of Hoblic Schools Started in 1868-69.

TABLE 2

District-Wise Schools

District	*No. of Schools*
Kolar	39
Bangalore	23
Tumkur	13
Mysore	30
Shimoga	5
Hassan	16
Kadur	10
Chitradurga	8

Excepting in schools in Kolar Mysore and Kadur districts, Panchayats were not constituted in Hobli Schools, In these Panchayats the Gowda, Shanubhoga, Merchants leading ryots,

Bahmins and in, some case pensioners functioned. Over the years the government started more of these schools so that by 1879-80, there were 636 schools and by 1899-1900 there were 1376 schools in the state. But as seen from Table 3, the growth was not uniform in all the districts the records do not explain this lopsided development.

TABLE 3

Districts and Hobli Schools

Sl.No.	*Name of the District*	*Number of Hobli Schools*	
		1879-1880	*1899-1900*
1.	Bangalore	99	244
2.	Kolar	105	216
3.	Tumkur	65	171
4.	Mysore	108	264
5.	Hassan	69	114
6.	Shimoga	72	172
7.	Kadur	56	59
8.	Chitradurg	62	136
	Total	636	1376

Further these schools were not as popular as made out by the Government and all the enthusiasm seems to have been only in the first few years. Again, going by attendance figures for a few years even it can be seen these generally more Hindu children attended these schools than Muslims children or children of Panchama caste groups. Again while it is rightly pointed out that Panchama children were kept out of these schools it is difficult to understand why Muslim children too did not go to these schools as did the Hindu children. Table 4 gives the details of Hindu Muslim and Panchama children attending the Hobli schools for several years.

TABLE 4

Showing Pupils in Hobli Schools by Religion/Caste for Several Years

	1870 - 72			1871 - 72			1872 - 73			1873 - 74			1874 - 75			1875 - 76			1876 - 77			1877 - 78		
	H	M	O	H	M	O	H	M	O	H	M	O	H	M	O	H	M	O	H	M	O	H	M	O
Tumkur-Dist	1299	—	—	1608	84	34	1474	60	—	1251	50	—	1673	61	—	2042	106	—	2195	66	—	1797	82	—
Mysore-Dist	1499	27	—	2069	41	1	1838	68	1	1975	68	3	2326	96	10	2579	109	—	3273	188	—	2809	188	—
Hassan-Dist	1230	—	—	1570	165	—	1573	36	—	1537	39	—	1803	51	—	1942	50	—	2073	17	—	1417	8	—
Shimoga-Dist	754	27	40	81	35	—	1195	26	—	1247	59	—	1511	56	17	2185	78	—	2365	56	10	2156	47	—
Kadur-Dist	496	21	—	728	33	—	811	33	—	834	29	—	1113	56	9	1291	64	6	1534	62	9	1284	210	0
Chitradurga Dist.	378	—	—	773	2	—	1307	—	—	1106	92	—	1114	89	18	2051	113	8	1890	100	12	1489	77	18
Bangalore Dist.	1365	80	—	1864	75	—	1757	76	—	1812	102	6	2217	25	7	2711	193	5	2944	175	4	2507	8	3
Kolar Dist.	1733	130	—	1608	184	34	1623	106	10	1624	136	17	2078	238	13	2226	273	16	2283	226	—	2234	163	15

In 1869-70 the records show that in addition to Brahmins children, those of cultivator, labourers, ryots and fishermen classes attended these schools. In the Hobli schools there were 5 classes from 1 to 5. In the lowest or first of these, children learnt to read letters of the vernacular off cards or formed letters with their fingers on the sand. In the next higher class the children used the first reading book in Kannada with short words and sentences, learnt, to use a slate, write numerals in Kannada or English and read numbers by 10s and so on. In the third class they learnt, to read short stories to give meaning of phrases, write to dictation, orthography in grammar and learnt multiplication tables including fractions worked on simple arithmetic and to point to principal features on a map the world. In the fourth class children learnt advanced reading, higher poetry, writing to dictation. On paper, reading manuscripts, learnt, parts of speech, recited from memory portions of Amarakosa, learnt sums in compound arithmetic and pointed to countries of the world with cities on a map. In the 5th or highest class children learnt selections of poetry and difficult prose, learnt lessons in agriculture and sanitary subjects, wrote petitions and letters, learnt lesions in agriculture, and sanitary subjects, wrote petitions and letters, learnt syntax in grammar, Amarakosa, proportion and interest in arithmetic measurement, accounting, learnt natural features, products population of different nations of the world especially of India.

Female Education

As already noted the Hobli school scheme was proposed in response to a note from the government of India that, there were no schools for female children in Mysore. This note referred only to the absence of Government Schools for female children. Table below gives the data for Government Girls School between 1869-70 and 1877-78.

TABLE 5

Enrolment of Children

Year	No. of Schools	Total Children
1869-70	5	136
1870-71	5	153
1871-72	5	237
1872-73	8	242
1873-74	9	252
1874-75	9	337
1875-76	9	346
1876-77	11	354
1877-78	11	468

Available data also reveals that nearly 97% of these were Hindu children while the rest were Muslims. Further a large percentage of these female children were from Bangalore

On the other hand it is significant that the earliest school for female children in the grant-in-aid category was started in 1840 in Etchinapalli. This was called the Madrasa Ibrahim. By 1871-72 the following were the various schools for female children in the state.

TABLE 6

Establishment of Schools

Name	Location	Year of Starting
Lower Class (Primary)		
St.Marks Ragged School	Bangalore	1854
Anglo Vernacular		
Blackpalli Catholic School	Bangalore	1862
Catholic School	Mysore	1861
Madrasa Mohemedia	Bangalore	1862

Name	*Location*	*Year of Starting*
Vernacular School		
Bangalore Sanskrit School	Bangalore	1870
Balckpalli Catholic School	-"-	1865
Commissariat Hindustan School	-"-	1864
Chintamani Sanskrit School	Chintamani	1868
Chikkaballapur Sanskrit School	Chikballapur	1865
Closepet Hindustani School	Closepet	1864
Chatnahalli Kanarese School	Singapur	1868
Doddaballapur Hindustani School	Doddaballapur	1868
Gun Troop Tamil School	Bangalore	1864
Honnali Hindustani School	Honnali	1869
Huliyurdurga Hindustani School	Huliyurdurga	1869
Kunnigallu Hindustani School	Kunnigallu	1864
Kalasa Kanarese School	Kalasa	1864
Madrasa Ahmedia	Srirangapatna	1865
Madrasa Islamia	Bangalore	1860
-"- Islamia	Chintamani	1856
-"- Ibrahim	Etchinapalli	1840
-"- Kuddesaa	Bangalore	1863
-"- Mohamedia	Channapatna	1864
-"- Alahomedia	French Rooks	1865
-"- Sultania	Bangalore	1866
-"- Sultania	Hunasuru	1866
Melukote Sanskrit School	Melukote	1862
Ronur Hindustani School	Ronur	1868
Magadi Sanskrit School	Magadi	1870
Sadarveda Siddamata Sabha School	Bangalore	1842
Srirangapatna Sanskrit School	Srirangapatna	1869
Shettahalli Catholic School	Shettahalli	1862
Hassan Hindustani School	Hassan	1866

contd...

Name	Location	Year of Starting
Tyamagondlu Hindustani School	Tyamagondlu	1868
Wesleyan Mission Peta School	Bangalore	1859
Wesleyan Mission Market School	Mysore	1866
Wesleyan Mission Mysore School	Mysore	1857
Wesleyan Mission School Tumkur Fort	Tumkur	1842
Weslyan Mission School Kytasandra	Kytasandra	1861
Weslyan Mission School Gubbi	Gubbi	1840
Weslyan Mission School Hosahalli	Hosahalli	1843
Weslyan Mission School Kolluru	Kolluru	1860
Weslyan Mission School Shimoga	Shimoga	1866
Weslyan Mission School Kunigallu	Kunigallu	1871

The next Table gives the data regarding female children attending the grant-in-aid schools between 1869-70 and 1877-78.

TABLE 7

Total No. of Pupils

Year	No. of schools	No. of Pupils
1869-70	28	2959
1870-71	33	2100
1871-72	45	2919
1872-73	28	2098
1873-74	29	2033
1874-75	25	1685
1875-76	33	1495
1876-77	34	2754
1877-78	39	2959

Achievements : 1854-1868

By the time the Hobli Schools scheme came into operation in 1868 there were a total of 110 institutions for Primary education in the state of these 64 were Government schools and 46 schools were aided by the Government. In these institution there were totally 6935 children of whom 3634 were boys and 1301 were girls. The Table below gives the break up of these figures in 1868.

TABLE 8

No. of Government and Grant in Aid Schools

Govt. Schools	*Pupils*	*Grant-in-aid schools*	*Pupils*
High Schools 8	1104	4	671
Middle Schools 9	278	6	359
Primary Schools 45	1363	20	1807
Female Schools	—	16	1301

These figures make obvious that while there were more schools started by Government, Pupils by and large went to the Grant-in-aid schools. Secondly, it is very interesting to observe that while only 18.75% of the total schools going children in the state were females and all of them went to Grant-in-aid schools. The records reveal that several schools displayed little vitality and in many cases the students showed very little interest in the subjects taught. Further it is also significant that most of these children were Hindus while Muslims and Panchama children took the second and third places respectively.

After 1900, the Hobli Schools Scheme began to stagnate. The number of Hobli Schools in the state increased to 1385 in 1900-1901, and declined to 1316 in 1901-02 Again it rose to 1364 the next year declined to 1350 in 1903-04, increased to 1352 schools the next year and declined during the two following years. After 1907-08 the reports do not specifically return the Hobli Schools under that name and they are classed as Village Elementary schools.

Compulsory Education Scheme (1913)

After the Hobli Schools scheme, till 1913 the Government did not undertake any specific scheme for the development of Primary Education. Infact between 1900 and 1907 Primary Education in Mysore state was not at all improving for, there was only an increase of 7 schools totally. Attendance in these schools was very bad and was accounted for by the prevalence of epidemic diseases in many places in the state over these years.

In 1907, the Government considered starting atleast one primary school in every village with a population of 300 for hardly 41.5% of such villages had schools in the state. That year the inspector general of education proposed the total abolition of fees in the primary classes entirely and enhancing teachers salaries. But during the next few years, in spite of these proposals being brought into effect the attendance of children improved population very slowly. In 1914 the government noted that of a total as of 58 lakhs., 18% were in the Primary school age at 8.7 lakhs. of these only 12500 children were actually under instruction. The Government thought of an ambitious scheme of providing for schools for 40000 children which meant starting of 4000 schools. But when it came to finances for this grand scheme it had to be given up.

Meanwhile in 1913 the Government brought into effect the Compulsory Primary Education Scheme. This scheme was initially started in 15 centres where by some 1200 more children in addition to the 10800 boys in the ages of 7-11 years already in school would attend school. In 1916-17, the scheme was extended to 168 of which 28 were in Bangalore, 17 in Shimoga, 16 in Chitradurga, 13 in Kolar, 34 in Myosre, 35 in Tumkur, 12 in Hassan and 13 in Kadur districts. By 1917 the Government was optimistic for it said the scheme has how passed the stage of experiment and many of the preliminary difficulties have been overcome. It should be organized on a proper permanent basis in the light of the experience gained and the entire responsibilities for its working be transferred to the local authorities and agencies. But this optimism was short lived for the very next year C.R. Reddy commented very appropriately that compulsory education would be truly beneficial only if it were made voluntary. Secondly, he came down heavily on the uneven distribution of schools under the scheme and the stress or bias in favour of schools in urban areas and especially in Bangalore, Tumkur and Mysore districts. Further he also appositely observed that this scheme, would be very expensive for the social conditions in the country (Mysore state) necessitated separate schools for various caste groups particularly panchamas and muslims. By 1920 this scheme suffered a setback. The long passage quoted below from the Report on public instruction of the year 1920 brings out the problems involved in the scheme.

During recent tours we noticed that many of the attendance committees were not working properly and in accordance with the rules laid down by Government for their guidance; and I, therefore, caused an investigation to be made. From the details supplied regarding the 62 committees it was found that only 11 (in the Shimoga District and 2 in Hassan) met once a month in accordance with the rules. 10 met seven times during the year. 11 six times, 10 twice, 2 once; and 9 did not meet at all. The statistics of attendance are not more satisfactory either. Some time out of 12 members, Only two were present and though the rules provide for the deletion of the names of those who do not attend regularly, still absentee membership is not so rare as it ought to be. Some members attended only once during the year; some twice; some thrice and so on; and a critical review of the details show that only one member was present for all the meetings. The vast majority of those who attend regularly are officials. A strict enforcement of the rules of membership is desirable if they are to be rejuvenated. At present the duties of attendance officers are entrusted in the vast majority of cases to Educational officers, who are, doing their best in a difficult situation which is subject to many limitations. In the first place, the enforcement of compulsion and the penal clauses of the scheme especially requires a certain amount of enlightened popular support; and perhaps also a higher official status for the enforcing officer. It is not easy to suggest a remedy for this weakness in our compulsory system, but the progress of education and the improvement in the public spirit of the people which time and education many bring about will, in due course, supply the remedy. The table below clearly shows the failure of the scheme.

The several defects of the present compulsory education scheme were detailed in the Educational Memorandum and final orders of Government are awaited.

The scheme of Compulsory Education for girls was not introduced in other centers besides the two cities of Bangalore and Mysore, where the Compulsory Education of girls is now under the control of the Inspector-General.

In the whole state, the scheme is in operation 240 centres. A sum of Rs.400 was granted towards the cost of taking Census. During the year under report, 9379 boys and 2188 girls of compulsory ages were admitted, 2807 warnings were issued and 116 prosecutions instituted. No new centers were selected during the year, and Government Orders on the policy of Education are awaited regarding the extension of the Scheme.

The most pressing wants of the schools already opened under the Scheme were met out of the general allotment of Rs.65000 for additional requirements as no separate allotment was earmarked for the purpose.

TABLE 9

Compulsory Primary Education Progress Under the Mysore Elementary Education Regulation V, 1913

Years	*No. of boys in Primary staged*	*No. of Centres*	*No. of New Schools*	*No. Induced to attend*	*No. of Warning notices issued*	*No. of Prosecutions*	*No. of Convictions*
1910 - 11	74,668	—	—	—	—	—	—
1911 - 12	79,658	—	—	—	—	—	—
1912 - 13	83,875	—	—	—	—	—	—
1913 - 14	Not available	15	—	—	—	—	—
1914 - 15	1,26,664	15	26	1200	—	—	—
1915 - 16	1,43,736	27	4	3600	82	—	—
1916 - 17	1,95,076	68	44	8086	1389	—	—
1917 - 18	2,13,984	136	92	1,2707	1972	11	—
1918 - 19	2,05,552	220	20	1,1407	1879	34	4
1919 - 20	2,01,202	220	N.A	—	1658	72	38
1920 - 21	1,82,956	220	—	—	—	—	—
1921 - 22	1,60,339	220	—	—	—	—	—
1922 - 23	1,80,755	220	—	—	—	—	—

In order to justify compulsion in the case of very poor students of the Depressed classes whose parents cannot afford to buy books and slates, the Government allotted Rs.5,000/- for the purchase of books and slates.

Additional grants amounting to Rs.6184 were also sanctioned to Primary Schools under Compulsory Education Scheme at Mysore City. In Government Order No.11307-8-Edn. 59-19-20 of 31st May 1920. The table below clearly shows the failure of the scheme.

TABLE 10

Aided Primary School Converted into Government Primary Schools

District	*No. of Schools Converted*	*No. of Fresh Schools Started*	*Year of Activity*
Bangalore	141	44	1922, 23, 25, 29, 30
Chitradurga	100	53	1923, 24, 25, 28, 30, 31
Shimoga	146	52	1924, 26, 27, 28, 29, 31
Hassan	151	111	1925, 26, 27, 28, 29, 30, 31
Tumkur	149	19	1925
Mysore	159	254	1927, 28, 29
Kadur	101	82	1928, 1929, 30
Kolar	129	205	1930, 31

1921 to 1931

Following on the Government orders on the Education Memorandum the Department of Public Instruction ordered an Educational Census of the state. On the basis of the data from this census and on the basis of the recommendations of the Memorandum the Department began converting aided Primary Schools into Government, Primary schools. The Table 10 shows the schools converted under this proposal. The conversion was to be based on the criteria of the schools serving a large section of population. Secondly from 1 July

1923 Middle schools were bifurcated from Primary Schools and Primary schools were to have 4 years course. Between 1921 and 1931 a large number of schools were started and generally more girls entered these schools. Further it is also interesting that girls generally went to schools under private management. The Table 11 below gives these details.

TABLE 11

Year	*School under public Management*		*School under private management*		*Total schools*	*No. of girls in schools*
	No. of Schools	*Pupils*	*No. of Schools*	*Pupils*	—	—
1921-22	2062	90793	—	84405	6216	14902
1926-27	3767	173787	1891	50585	5658	21512
1931-32	4434	174686	1242	36258	3676	23482

But during these years there was another development namely retardation and wastage, otherwise called 'dropping out'. A large number of children dropped out after the 1st of Primary Schools. The table below gives the details of wastage for several year.

TABLE 12

Dropping Out Children

Year	*Between 1-2 yrs*	*Between 2-3-yrs*	*Between 3-4 yrs*	*Between 4-17 yrs*
1928-29	61991	23127	25152	11965
1929-30	84824	7778	8289	22287
1930-31	88103	10443	9778	11484
1931-32	67829	12810	10849	10012

Government attempted to assess the causes of this wastage and give at the following conclusion: (1) apathy of people towards education and poverty (2) irregular attendance and admission all round the year (3) predominance of single teacher schools and large classes (4) shortness of school course and (5) Unsuitability of curriculum (6) inadequately qualified teachers. Of these factors only the first is really correct and the rest are obviously only incidental. The government noted that this wastage and retardation was distressingly heavy and that the expenditure was not getting the correspondency results.

TABLE 13

Percentage of Boys in Primary Schools

Years	*% of Boys in 1 year of Primary School to total in 4 primary classes*
1927-28	46.1
1928-29	58.2
1929-30	57.11
1930-31	54.57
1931-32	52.42

1931-1941

From as far back as 1883 the Government had been considering the question of transferring Primary Education to local bodies. While the Government several times advanced the view that this would make the local bodies strong, and they could also control and direct the funds. That they were contributing as local cess to the state the actual motive was different primary education was not producing the results expected and Government felt that this was burden some to the state exchequer. Hence under the elementary education Act 1931 responsibility of Primary Education was transferred to the Local Education Authorities one each for the 8 districts and 4 large municipalities of Kolar gold fields, Mysore city, Bangalore and Tumkur. The L.E.A. was responsible for the Management of Schools under its custody in all matters of policy and finance L.E.A. was to confirm to standards fixed by Govt. and Noncompliance would result in forfeiture of this power. In 1931, totally 6173 schools all over the state were transferred to LEA's as shown below.

TABLE 14

District Boards	Bangalore	-793
	Kolar	-750
	Shimoga	-775
	Kadur	-453
	Mysore	-1296
	Tumkur	-813
	Chitradurga	-509
	Hassan	-626
Cities	Bangalore City	-53
	K.G.F	-42
	Mysore	-52
	Tumkur Town	-11
		6173

But quickly this scheme became ineffective. Every year in several LEA's a number of schools became dysfunctional mainly due to lack of funds. The Table below gives the details of this retardation in Primary education in Mysore State between 1931-1941.

As in the earlier years wastage and retardation was high at the I year of the Primary classes itself to remedy these defects a committee was appointed to inquire into the entire education system in the state below the University stage and on the basis of its recommendations the Elementary Education Act 1941, which completely with drew the 1931 scheme was introduced.

TABLE 15

Enrolment of Boys and Girls

Years	Boys		Girls	
	School	Pupils	School	Pupils
1930-31	5857	222816	538	31443
1931-32	5676	222816	523	31443
1932-33	5706	210944	537	31297
1933-34	5718	214997	536	322294
1934-35	5735	213802	515	32471
1935-36	5783	216721	503	32857
1936-37	5868	217063	481	33197
1937-38	5919	213684	473	33415
1939-40	6025	239650	462	34683
1940-41	6050	239263	—	—

Female Education

While female children began entering schools, till very late in the twentieth century. There was great reluctance and even opposition from various quarters to efforts in this directions. The Reports of Public Instruction particularly of the last quarter of the last century give interesting information on the reaction and situation of female education. In 1868-69 the report observed that most of the children belonged to the Brahmin community came from affluent urban families. In 1878-79, the department noted that, girls schools were "exotic" institutions and that they laboured from want of female teachers. In 1888-89 the report noted that fear of conversion to Christianity was one of the reasons for female children not being sent to schools particularly aided schools. Even in 1900 it was noted that enforcement of attendance was impossible in girls schools.

Later as the backward class movement gained momentum the view was expressed that spending money of female education was incorrect when a large section of society consisting of backward and depressed classes were not educated at all. This situation continued practically till the 1930 as seen from the report on public instruction in the state for that year.

3

Growth of Secondary Education in Mysore Princely State

Secondary education could be broadly defined as the process of schooling beyond the primary stage and terminating with the examination even now described as the secondary school leaving certificate. This consists of two areas, the first, Middle School stage and the second the High School stage.

Middle Schools

The Middle School stage began from the fifth year of education, which was the stage where Primary Education terminated and ended with the eighth year. Obviously the Middle School consisted of four years from the 5th to the 8th. Practically till 1923 the Middle Schools were attached to Primary Schools. That year they were bifurcated as separate entities. But till 1923 they were usually described as Lower Secondary, Higher Primary or Middle School stages. Thus in the present study middle Schools are not studied as a part of the Primary School system but they are treated as a distinct section of the Secondary Education system.

Under the category called middle schools there were two types of schools (1) Inferior Anglo Vernacular Schools and (2) Vernacular Schools. The Inferior Anglo vernacular Schools which were situated in the taluk headquarter towns were giving, as their nomenclature indicates, instruction in the English language in addition to other subjects. The second category, were more or less continuations of Primary Schools, where, no instruction in English was given.

The Inferior Anglo Vernacular Schools were by no means popular. Further, the Government of the day too, considered these institutions as expensive and did not look upon them, Kindly. The reason was that the standard of English taught as a language was bad. Good teachers of English were not available. Infact in 1873-74 when B.L. Rice, Director of Public Instruction proposed starting Vernacular schools in taluk towns where English would be taught on public demand, if the people (parents) agreed to bear the expenditure for a good English teacher the Chief Commissioner opposed the scheme. His arguments were that those classes which would be attracted by this scheme would expect Government employment for which English knowledge was necessary but such hopes would remain unfulfilled for good English teachers were not available to work in taluk towns. As seen from the Table 16 the number of Inferior Anglo Vernacular Schools began to decline middle between 1868 and 1877.

TABLE 16

Inferior Anglo-Vernacular Schools

Departmental			*Aided*				*Total*	
			Boys		*Girls*			
Year	*No.*	*Strength*	*No.*	*Strength*	*No.*	*Strength*	*No.*	*Strength*
1868-69	10	231	8	556	2	138	20	925
1872-73	6	222	9	629	4	191	19	1042
1876-77	5	183	7	449	3	113	15	745

Vernacular Schools

After the establishment of the Department of Public Instruction in the State in 1857, a proposal was sent up to the

TABLE 17

Vernacular Schools 1871 - 72

	Government			*Aided*			*Total*		
Name of District	*No. of Schools*	*Total Strength*	*Average Attendance*	*No. of Schools*	*Total Strength*	*Average Attendance*	*No. of Schools*	*Total Strength*	*Average Attendance*
Bangalore	15	731	572	30	2426	1962	45	3157	2534
Kolar	17	724	490	5	174	143	22	796	633
Tumkur	10	499	391	8	457	351	18	956	742
Mysore	13	761	549	10	697	505	23	1458	1054
Hassan	11	372	300	1	40	37	12	412	337
Shimoga	10	518	425	3	111	94	13	629	519
Kadur	8	261	223	1	10	9	9	271	232
Chitradurga	11	435	334	—	—	—	11	435	334
Total	95	4201	3284	58	3915	3101	153	8116	6385

Government of India for starting Middle School described as Vernacular Schools at the taluk head quarter towns. These schools were to be started on the basis of public demand for the same after the scheme was sufficiently advertised by the department. If sufficient applications were not forth coming, Government, was to start such schools by itself on an experimental basis. Even after this, if such schools were not well received by the people, notices were to be put up explaining that only persons educated in these schools would be eligible for Government employment in the salary of Rs.6 and above per month.

However the demand for such schools came slowly. Fifteen applications alone came between 1859-60 and by 1863 there were only 8 such schools in the state. Since several schools closed down. And by 1871-72, there were 93 schools all over the state.

However as seen from the Table below, as in the case of Primary Schools, Aided Vernacular schools were better than the Government Vernacular Schools in all respects.

As in the case of Primary Schools there was considerable wastage and retardation. In a large majority of these schools, all the four classes did not exist. Rather children were found to drop out at the end of the first year of the Middle School level. Data regarding dropping out of children and consequent closure of schools for want of pupils for the years 1857-1868 is not available. But the position between 1868-1873 is very interesting and presented in the below Table.

Attendance was also very poor and the Government naturally felt it was waste of money to increase more of these Middle Schools several efforts were made between 1873 and 1900 to put the Middle Schools of both categories on some firm footing and they generally failed. In 1894 the Government made an important modification in the two categories of

Middle Schools that then existed. They were hence forth to be named Vernacular and Anglo Vernacular Middle Schools.

TABLE 18

Position of Taluk Vernacular Schools (1873-74)

Grade	*No. of Schools which had reached the standard of*			
	Kannada	*Telugu*	*Hindustani*	*Total*
I Year	12	—	—	12
II Year	46	2	5	53
III year	23	3	6	32
IV Year	—	1	6	7
Total	81	6	17	104

Until 1921 when Government passed orders on the Education Memorandum, Middle School education progressed on the lines of two categories of schools above described with the distinction that in one category English was taught as a subject while, in the other, it was purely instruction in the Vernacular.

But, gradually it was found that a few candidates now and then passed out of the Vernacular Middle Schools and wanted to enter the High Schools. They were not eligible, for to enter High Schools pupils had to have studied English language as a subject at the Middle level. To help such candidates it was provided that they had to pass through four years of schooling additionally at the middle level studying and passing only in English as a subject. This provision obviously cost a pupil time and energy at an important stage in his life. But nothing was done to remedy the situation.

1921 to 1941

According to the Government orders on the Education Memorandum (1) there was to be no distinction between

Vernacular and Anglo Vernacular Middle Schools. (2) the medium of instruction at Middle Schools was to be uniformly in the Vernacular, English being taught as a compulsory language. (3) Middle schools were to provide instruction for 4 years and (4) Primary Schools which had been giving instruction in Middle School levels were to be separated.

But financial stringency prohibited Government from putting into effect these orders. Hence the Anglo Vernacular schools which had 15 pupils in the 3rd and 4th classes, were split as incomplete Middle Schools and they were to provide instruction in English from the 2nd year of the Middle stage. It was proposed that as funds became available these schools would be fully instructing in English as a language. For a time these incomplete Middle schools were popular and in demand in rural areas particularly. But gradually they proved unsuccessful as children, Who came thorough these schools failed to pass the examination at the end of the Middle stage. Thus practically till 1940 as seen from the table below when the present study ends middle school education continued in a state of confusion.

TABLE 19

Growth of Schools in Mysore

Showing the Growth of Middle Schools

Years	*Schools for boys*	*Schools for girls*
1924	215	23
1925	205	22
1926	215	23
1927	235	22
1928	252	25
1929	252	25
1930	259	26
1931	284	28
1935	293	35
1936	293	33

Middle School Examination

Until 1876 there was no public examination at the end of the Middle School level. In March that year the following order which was an announcement of a public examination was published. "From and after 1st April 1876, no person not being a matriculated student of any University, or not having passed the Madras general Test, or who has not been continuously employed in the public service since January 1860, shall be appointed to any situation under the Mysore government the salary of which may exceed Rs. 20 a month without having passed a satisfactory examination in the following subjects.

a) Hand writing, including ability to copy within a prescribed time and in a good clear hand manuscript or printed paper.
b) Orthography to include writing from dictation and correctly re-writing a misspelt passage
c) Composition and Grammer, including ability to write a single letter in good grammatical style and to answer questions on grammer.
d) Arithmetic, the first four rules, simple and compound vulgar and decimal fractions and questions involving the rule of three.
e) Geography including the elements of General Geography and a somewhat more accurate knowledge of Geography of India and Mysore in particular.
f) History including knowledge of the leading facts of the history of India and Mysore in particular.

The examination will be divided into two branches, English and Kanarese Candidates for employment in an appointment the duties of which require a knowledge of English, will be required to execute the tests in hand writing, Orthography, composition and grammer in the English language. All candidates will be required to perform the test in Arithmetic, Geography and History in Kanarese.

The examinations provided for in these rules shall be conducted by means of printed papers. They shall be open to all candidates whose age exceeds 17 years on the 1st of October of the year in which the examination is held.

The examination will be held annually in the month of November at the under mentioned places. Bangalore, Mysore, Shimoga, A fee of Rs.4 will be required from all candidates. This fee will be paid by each candidate into a taluk Treasury, and they will grant him a receipt.

All applications from candidates desirous of appearing at the above mentioned examinations must be addressed to the Director of Public Instructions, Bangalore in time to reach him not later than October 1st Each application must be accompanied by the following certificates.

1. A certificate from a Civil surgeon, that the applicant is of sound bodily health and free grom constitutional infirmity unfitting him for the services of government.
2. A Certificate from an Amildar that the applicant has paid the prescribed fee of Rs.4 into the Taluk Treasury.
3. Evidence that the applicant will be more than 17 years of age on the 1st October of the year in which the examination is held.

The Chief Commissioner reserves to himself the power of exempting any candidate for Government employment from the necessity of passing the test, but such exemptions will only be granted in very special cases.

This was the Madras Middle School Examination Later in 1886, the Mysore Government instituted the Mysore Local Examination for pupils taking the Vernacular Middle School

Courses. The difference in examination was that in the latter the examination were in Vernacular. From December 1891 both these examinations were given up and their place was taken by the Mysore Lower Secondary Examination. This was common for both pupils of Anglo Vernacular and Vernacular Middle Schools. But while it was optional for the latter category, it was compulsory further former category because they would after passing this examination enter High Schools.

Over the years, however, more pupils from the Vernacular Middle Schools took this examination and were successful when compared with pupils from anglo Vernacular Middle Schools. After 1891 there was no significant change in the Middle School examination scheme will the period when the present study closes.

Higher Secondary Education

In continuation of the Middle School Education was the Higher Secondary Education. As in the case of the Middle Schools in Mysore State Higher Secondary education also had two distinct and differently oriented branches. They were the Upper Secondary Scheme and the English High School Scheme. The former was a two year Vernacular scheme in continuation of the Vernacular Middle School Scheme. The latter was a three year scheme in continuation of the Anglo-Vernacular Middle School Scheme. The former terminated with an examination following which there was a one year Upper Secondary Training Course. A pupil obtaining a certificate at this training course could be in employed as a teacher in a vernacular Middle school or with further instruction in Sanskrit or Urdu could become a pandit or moulvi in a High School. The three year High School Scheme terminated with the Secondary School leaving Certificate which entitled a person to seek employment in the Government at the clerical levels. But schools offering this upper secondary course in Mysore state were very few. Further these schools were not popular either. In 1918-19, the inspector General of Education realistically observed that this upper secondary course peculiar to Mysore State parallely run with a English High School scheme was like a mixture of cloud and moon shine," a costly failure" and hence had to be given up. Finally in 1934, a new course called vernacular Teachers Certificate course was started and the upper secondary courses were abolished.

High Schools Upto 1941

These institutions were also called English High Schools. Entry to the High School was given to the pupils who had passed the Lower Secondary Examination in a Anglo – Vernacular Middle School. But often this was not insisted if the candidate had passed the English language Examination at the Middle school.

TABLE 20

Type of Schools and Enrolment of Students

		Government		*Aided*		*Total*	
Years		*Institutions*	*No. of Scholars*	*Institutes*	*No. of Scholars*	*Institutions*	*No. of Scholars*
1868-69	Boys	8	982	5	781	13	1763
	Girls	—	—	—	—		
1879-80	Boys	11	422	9	373	22	816
	Girls	—	—	2	21	—	—
1889-90	Boys	10	1292	3	1343	11	2635
	Girls	—	—	—	—	—	
1899-	Boys	10	3165	3	1373	14	4550
1900	Girls	1	12	—	—	—	—

The course in the High School was of three years duration. Until 1913 the candidates who had undergone this course were entitled to take the Madras Matriculation Examination conducted by Madras University. The year the Secondary School Leaving Certificate Scheme was introduced.

Very early, Examination was considered as interfering with the studies of pupil because several subjects such as natural philosophy and literature studied by pupils were not subjects for Examination at all. The reason was the Examination was designed to give the pupil the basic needs for becoming a government clerk. The table below shows the development of High Schools between 1868-1900.

This Table indicates another interesting feature, that most of the entrants to these schools were boys because for the girls the S.S.L.C. was only a qualification to be had for its own sake. Even as late as in 1915-16 as seen from Table, 21 the percentage of girls was not very remarkable. There was slow improvement after 1916.

TABLE 21

No. of Boys and Girls in High School

Years	*Boys*	*Girls*
1910-11	25871	7510
1915-16	33081	10984

Again a major percentage of pupils in these schools were Brahmins as seen in table 22. This position also changed gradually over the years after 1920.

TABLE 22

Caste Wise Break up of Students

	1910-11	*1915-16*
Brahmin	3146	3607
Non-Brahmin Hindu	—	1351
Christian	131	149
Panchamas	25	71
Muslims	126	228
Europeans	7	6

4

Educational Policy and Legislation

Developments from 1800 to 1854

While the princely state of Mysore came under the web of British Paramountcy way back in 1799, it was not until half a century afterwards that some steps were taken which could be identified as educational policy. The English East India Company was basically interested in augmenting the revenues of its subsidiary ally and reorganizing or gearing up the administration with a view to the effective realization of the Subsidy due to it under the conditions of the Subsidiary Treaty of 1799. In fact, in the huge quantity of official discussion till the 1830s there is practically no reference to the subject of education at all.

In 1831 after the Nagar disturbances, the East India Company took over the administration of the State and set aside the Maharaja Krishna Raja Wodeyar III. The State consequently came under direct British rule. One of the earliest references to education in the state by a British visitor dates back to 1824. In this note, the visitor observed, that the state of education in Mysore was definitely much inferior to what obtained in the Madras Presidency. As already observed, in 1830 the first modern school was established in Bangalore. But sequestration of the administration did not mean anything so far as education was concerned in the State. Until 1854, the development of education consisted merely in starting a few schools mainly to cater to the needs of the children of soldiers of the military force. These efforts were not systematic either.

In 1854 which is a bench mark in the history of modern education in India, the East India Company issue the famous Halifax Dispatch. A few paras from this much quoted and discussed document would not be out of place here.

It appears to us that the present time, when by an Act of the Imperial Legislature the responsible trust of Government of India has again been placed in our hands, is peculiarly suitable for the review of the progress which has already been made, the supply of existing deficiencies, and the adoption of such improvements as may be best calculated to secure the ultimate benefit of the people committed to our charge.

Among many subjects of importance, none can have a stronger claim to our attention than that of education. It is one of our most sacred duties to be the means, as far as in us lies, of conferring upon the natives of India those vast moral and material blessings which flow from the general diffusion of useful knowledge, and which India may, under Providence, derive from her connetion with England.

We have moreover, always looked upon the encouragement of education as peculiarly important, because calculated "not only to produce a higher degree of intellectual fitness, but to raise the moral character of those who partake of its advantages, and so to supply you with servants to whose probity you may with increased confidence commit offices of trust" in India, where the well-being of the people is so intimately connected with the truthfulness and ability of officers of every grade in all departments of the State.

Nor, while the character of England is deeply concerned

in the success of our efforts for the promotion of education, are her material interests altogether unaffected by the advance of European knowledge of India; this knowledge will teach the natives of India the marvelous results of the employment of labor and capital, rouse them to emulate us in the development of the vast resources of their country guide them in their efforts and gradually, but certainly, confer upon them all the advantages which accompany the healthy increase of wealth and commerce; and, at the same time, secure to us a larger and more certain supply of many articles necessary for our manufactures and extensively consumed by all classes of our population, as well as an almost inexhaustible demand for the produce of British labour.

We have from time to time given careful attention and encouragement to the efforts which have either to been made for the spread of education, and we have watched with deep interest the practical results of the various systems by which those efforts have been directed. The periodical reports of the different Councils and Boards of Education, together with other official communications upon the same subject have put us; in possession of full information as to those educational establishments which are under the direct control of Government; while the evidence taken before the Committees of both House of Parliament upon Indian affair has given us the advantage of similar information with respect to exertions made for this purpose by persons unconnected with government, and has also enabled us to profit by a knowledge of the views of those who are best able to arrive at sound conclusions upon the question of education generally.

We have next to consider the manner in which our object is to be effected, and this leads us to the question of the medium through which knowledge is to be conveyed to the people of India. It has hitherto been necessary, owing to the want of translations or adaptations of European works in the vernacular languages of India and to the very imperfect shape in which European knowledge is to be found in any works in the learned languages of the East, for those who desired to obtain a liberal education to begin by the mastery of the English language as a key to the literature of Europe, and a knowledge of English will always be essential to those natives of India who aspire to a high order of education.

In some parts of India, more especially in the immediate vicinity of the presidency towns, where persons who possess a knowledge of English are preferred to others in many employments, public as well as private, a very moderate proficiency in the English language is often looked upon by those who attend school instruction as the end and object of their education rather than as a necessary step to the improvement of their general knowledge. We do not deny the value in many respects of the mere faculty of speaking and writing English, but we fear that a tendency has been created in these districts unduly to neglect the study of the vernacular languages.

It is neither our aim nor desire to substitute the English language for the vernacular dialects of the country. We have always been most sensible of the importance of the use of the languages, which alone are understood by the great mass of the population. These languages, and not English, have been put by us in the place of Persian in the administration of justice and in the intercourse between the officers of Government and the people. It is indispensable, therefore, that, in any general system of education, the study of them should be assiduously attended to, and any acquaintance with improved European knowledge which is to be communicated to the great mass of the people whose circumstances prevent them from acquiring a high order of education, and who cannot be expected to overcome the difficulties of a foreign language can only be conveyed to them through one or other of those vernacular languages.

An adequate system of inspection will also, for the future, become an essential part of our educational system; and we desire that a sufficient number of qualified inspectors be appointed, who will periodically report upon the state of those colleges and schools which are now supported and managed by Government as well as of such as will hereafter be brought under Government inspection by the measures that we propose to adopt. They will conduct, or assist at, the examination of the scholars of these institutions, and generally, by their advice, aid the managers and school-masters in conducting colleges and schools of every description throughout the country. They will necessarily be of different classes, and may posses different degrees of acquirement, according to the higher or lower character of the institutions which they will be employed to visit; but we need hardly say that, even for the proper inspection of the lower schools, and with a view to their effectual improvement, the greatest care will be necessary to select persons of high character and fitting judgment for such employment. A proper staff of clerks and other officers will, moreover, be required for the Educational Departments.

Reports of the proceedings of the inspectors should be made periodically and these, again, should be embodied in the annual reports of the heads of the Educational Departments, which should be transmitted to us, together with statistical returns (to be drawn up in similar forms in all parts of India), and other information of a general character relating to education."

Devereux Scheme

Accordingly when the Woods Despatch was applied to

Mysore the then Judicial Commissioner of the State, Mr. Devereux prepared a scheme which was in consonance with it.

While forwarding this scheme to the Government of India Mark Cubbon observed, "it must be admitted that the administration of Mysore makes no particular show under the head of education. In an abstract point of view this is to be regretted, but subject nations are not kept in order and good humour on abstract principle and it has long been the opinion of some and is rapidly becoming the opinion of many, that the efforts which have been made by Government to extend the blessings of education and by tests and examinations to secure the services of enlightened men even in the lowest posts are not calculated to be so fully appreciated as they ought by any class of the community".

Under the Devereux scheme, the Department of Public Instruction was set up 1857. Regarding schools, it was proposed that under a Central College, four Anglo Vernacular schools in the Divisions one Vernacular School in each Taluk and two Normal Schools on each for the Malnad and Maidan areas of the State were to be set up. This education expansion programme was to be worked gradually and the optimum reached over several years. Fees were to be levied in all Government Schools. This extension programme worked slowly as noted above.

Hobli Schools Scheme 1868 – 1881

Meanwhile in 1868, the Government of India noted that schools for female children did not exist in the state and that more Vernacular schools were necessary. The director of Public Instruction B.L. Rice drew up the Hobli School Scheme. Rice summed up the progress achieved under Devereux Scheme and noted that a school in each taluk was not sufficient. Hence, "a school in each Hobli, a sub division of a taluk whereby even, the farthest village would not be more than 4 ½ miles from a school . . . ." was to be started. These Hobli schools were to be open to female children also. Further this scheme made detailed recommendations regarding expanding the supervision agency, an increase in salary to teachers, infrastructure and an annual budget. Regarding buildings, Rice suggested that as far as possible rent free buildings should be secured by informing the villagers regarding the usefulness of the schools. Perhaps the most important aspect of this scheme was that instruction was to be entirely in Kannada consisting of reading, writing and elementary arithmetic and geography. Very optimistically, Rice noted that if this scheme were adopted, the attendance of children at schools may go up to 50,000 from a paltry 1600 for the entire state in 1860 under the earlier scheme. Fees were to be collected from only those parents who did not contribute to the education fund under the local fund scheme of 1872. This scheme was to be explained to the people at large through notifications in Kannada. This scheme came into effect in 1868.

After 1868 education expanded, more schools, were started by popular demand more children in the school going age went to schools. More buildings were erected and more money was spent by the state authority on education. The records are full of this euphoria but careful study of the data reveals many aspects which would not admit of such praise for the achievements.

Basically between 1857 and 1900 for which period the above comment is relevant, the Government did not attempt to know the necessities of the people, in such an important area as education at the Primary and Secondary levels. Naturally all exercises consisted in an imposition from above without even the smallest semblance of understanding popular feelings. This is particularly clear in the matter of female education, which as noted earlier was not welcomed by the people generally.

1881 to 1912

Native rule was restored in 1881 under the terms of the Instrument of Transfer. This engagement did not specify any thing with regard to education. But it enjoined the ruler of Mysore not to alter the administrative system that existed in the state in 1881 without the sanction of the Governor-General in Council.

Addressing the first meeting of the Mysore Representative Assembly which had been founded in 1881 the Dewan C.V. Rangacharlu observed, "we are met here today by command of His Highness the Maharaja and it is His Highness' wish that I should place before you at these annual meetings a report of the administration of the past year and an outline of the measures proposed to be carried into effect in the coming year . . . ". But during the two years of Rangacharlu's Dewanship, the Government did not have any specific proposal or plan for the development of education in the state. Rangacharlu died in 1883 and was succeeded by K. Seshadri Iyer. But it was not till 1886 that Government directed its attention to the subject of education. As the biographer of Seshadri Iyer observes, "After the Restoration until 1886 due to financial exigencies not much could be done in the field of education". In 1886 addressing the Representative Assembly the Dewan observed that the policy of the Maharaja's Government regarding education aimed at the following ends; (1) efficient maintenance of elementary education and bringing it within reach of all classes of people; (2) to promote directly and indirectly through private agencies the growth of education; (3) to promote study of Vernaculars; (4) extend female education. This policy statement continued practically with no modification till 1912 when M. Visveswaraya became

Dewan. Further between 1881 and 1912 even in the Representative Assembly practically no significant questions were raised about education.

Dewanship of Visveswaraya (1912-1918)

In 1912 M.Visveswaraya, one of the brilliant minds of that period became Dewan of Mysore. An engineer by training he had visited the west and had been deeply impressed by the developments in Europe. Indirectly he came under the influence of the neo classical growth model economists of the west and sincerely sought to translate his ideas in Mysore. He aimed at the all round development of Mysore and education was one of the important subject which engaged the attention of this "developmentist". As in other fields he often compared developments in Mysore and the country in general with Europe and America statistically to drive home the point that India and Mysore lagged far behind.

According to Visveswaraya education was the sovereign remedy for all the ills faced by the nation. Addressing the students of Central College in 1912, he stated that statistically the 'development of education in Mysore was much better than that of all India figures but the progress was far from satisfactory. For while in the United States of America, the expenditure on education was as much as Rs. 12 per head of population, in Mysore it was just a few annas. He said, "Progress in every country depends mainly on the education of its people. Without education, we are a nation of children. The difference between one man and another apart from birth and social position, consists in the extent of knowledge, general and practical acquired by him. We may safely assume that men in all countries within certain limits start with the same degree of intelligence. A civilized nation is distinguished from an uncivilized one by the extent of its acquired intelligence and skill".

One year before he became Dewan, under Visveswaraya's guidance the Mysore Economic Conference a body, which aimed at the planned all round development of Mysore. Among the various objectives before the conference the promotion of education particularly elementary and secondary education was one. After its establishment the economic conference discussed several issues such as expansion of primary and secondary education, education of women, education of depressed and backward classes and so on. On all these issues, the Conference made recommendations to the Government. But, from the very time of its establishment, the Economic Conference was not very welcome. Its work was criticized by public men and the Press. Further within the administration also, there was opposition to the Conference. One of the most important achievements which came out of the deliberations of the Economic Conference was the establishment of the Mysore University in 1915.

Compulsory Elementary Education – 1913

In 1911 Gopalakrishna Gokhale had introduced a Bill for compulsory Elementary Education in the Imperial Legislative Council. This bill was based on the Irish Education Act (1892) and English Education Acts (1870) and (1876). Gokhale had spoken at length in the Council in 1911 that a beginning should be made in the direction of making Elementary Education free and compulsory throughout the country. The Bill proposed that Elementary Education should be made compulsory for boys between the ages of 6 and 11 years. This scheme was to be introduced gradually in selected centers. But finally, the Bill had been defeated in the Council.

In 1913 a Bill was introduced in the Mysore Representative Assembly closely resembling Gokhale's Bill After a brief debate, it was passed and became law that very year.

According to Regulation V of 1913:

1. Elementary education was defined as a course of reading writing and arithmetic (Section 2).
2. Parents had to send their male children compulsorily to schools between the ages of 7 and 11 years unless there was reasonable excuse for not attending (Section 3).
3. Boy's would be exempted from attending schools if,
   (a) There was no recognized school within 1 mile from the place of residence.
   (b) They were prevented from attending due to sickness infirmity, domestic necessity or seasonal needs.
   (c) They were receiving instruction in some suitable or satisfactory manner. (Section 4).

(4) Exemptions had to be granted by proper authority (Section 4d).

5. There was no compulsion to attend classes in religious instruction (Section 5).
6. Boys in the age group of 7 to 11 years were not be employed without exemption certificates from school (Section 6).
7. If parents failed in the first instance they could be fined Rs.2/- . (Section 8(a) If repeated parents would be fined Rs.10/- (Section 8 (b).
8. Persons who employed children between the ages of 7 and 11 years would be fined Rs. 20 (Section 9).

The statute provided that it could be extended to girls also. Rules under this law said that Elementary Education upto standard III was compulsory. Further boys had to attend school for 200 days in a year at 4 hours every day. Finally exemption certificates were valid only for 3 months at a time.

Backward Classes Movement and Education

It was during the Dewanship of Visweswaraya that the state witnessed the backward classes movement. This was a movement, the antecedents of which go back to the closing years of the Commissioner's rule in Mysore. It was essentially based on the argument that state in the public services of the state, there was a preponderance of the Brahmins. In fact this was noticed by Bowring and Seshadri Iyer. Later in 1917 a group of non Brahmin public men in Mysore, had formed the Praja Mitra Mandali the first organized party in the state with the express aim of promoting the interests of the backward classes. In 1981 under the directions of C.R. Reddy then Inspector General of Education in Mysore a delegation of the Mandali had met the Maharaja and presented a Memorandum.

In their Memorandum they observed that the Brahmins, preponderated in the state services. Further they appealed to the Maharaja to take steps to secure for the non Brahmins adequate representation in the Government services. More important, they urged the Maharaja to initiate steps to improve the educational level of the Non Brahmins particularly at the Secondary education level. The maharaja agreed in principle to the demands of the Mandali.

Following on these developments in August 1918, the Government appointed the Miller Committee giving them the following terms of reference.

(i) Any necessary changes in the existing rules of recruitment into public services, so that the adequate representation of backward classes in the state of services may be secured.

(ii) Special facilities to encourage high and professional education among the backward classes.

(iii) Special measures to secure increased representation of backward classes in the services without affecting efficiency. Measures for wider diffusion of education among backward classes.

The Miller Committee submitted its report two months later. On the subject of education they observed "generally a Education being the basic principle which tends to the harmonious equalization of the representation of the different communities in public services" earlier the committee justified its very appointment saying. "under the present system of Government, the officers of the government in the higher grades of services have necessarily much influence in shaping the policy of the administration and the efficiency of the services viewed as machines for securing the even and uniform progress of the state, is likely to be increased by the presence in their ranks of officers of different communities. And viewed from the point of view of the services themselves it is likely that their efficiency will be advanced by promoting greater feeling of equality among officers and by relieving those who are in the minority of the feeling that their interests are likely to suffer at the hands of the majority. For the fact cannot be ignored that an officer in the exercise of his duty making appointments and promotions finds its easier to see the virtues of his own community than those of others". A matter which is of importance and as to which we believe there exists some dissatisfaction is the question of the allotment of seats in schools and colleges. The refusal to admit the backward class students to a high schools or college class for want of accommodation is obviously a serious blow which may to an appreciable degree counteract any attraction towards higher education which the Government may provide. The discouragement caused to his community by the refusal to admit a backward class student is probably much higher in degree and more intense than would be caused to the Brahmin community by the rejection of a student of that class, and it is for this reason that the backward class students should receive a preferential treatment in this matter. We suggest that the claims of the backward communities should be satisfied first up to one-half of the number of seats available in each class or section thereof. And this should be done not over all the seats available as a whole but class by class to ensure that a member of the backward communities shall not unnecessarily be driven to study in a class which does not suit him. Such uneven distribution is suggested as it has been represented to us that some students of the backward classes have had to seek admission to aided schools in order to pursue studies in the mathematics and science sections. Owing to refusal of admission to those sections in Government Schools.

Earlier the committee defined all those communities in the state whose general literacy in English was less than 5% as backward. The committee recommended under Primary Education (1) special schools for depressed classes and general extension of Primary Education to benefit all backward classes. The Panchama schools were to have Panchama teachers. (2) Extension of scholarships to panchamas and backward classes. Regarding Secondary Education the Committee suggested increase of schools of the Anglo Vernacular type.

Elsewhere in the report, the committee recommended starting of Government hostels in all taluk headquarter towns to help the backward communities to send their children to these institutions to pursue Secondary education. This was particularly important in view of the fact that as the Committee observed that there was a fall in numbers after the completion of the Primary level. And the Committee reasoned that this fall was due to the non availability of Secondary schools in or near the villages. Further the committee suggested that 80% of seats in Government hostels should be reserved for backward classes. The committee said "a matter which is of importance and as to which we believe there exists some dissatisfaction is the question of the allotment of seats in schools and colleges. The refusal to admit the backward class students to a high schools or college class for want of accommodation is obviously a serious blow which may to an appreciable degree counteract any attraction towards higher education which the Government".

The Committee supported all these recommendations with detailed statistics. It noted the very negligible percentage of students of backward and panchama caste groups in hostels both private and managed by the state, the very meager percentage of students of non-brahmanic groups in primary and secondary schools, the very few freships and scholar ships granted to children of these communities and finally that meager member of persons of these groups in government services.

This report was kept in cold storage for two years and after a heated debate in the Representative Assembly orders were issued in 1921. Government accepted all the Recommendations of the committee regarding Education.

Educational Memorandum (1921)

The years following the introduction of the Compulsory Education Scheme were marked by stray efforts to, on the one hand increase, the number of schools and on the other hand to bring more schools under the Compulsory scheme. But both these line of effort were not as fruitful as they were expected to be. While government did not make any efforts to understand why these schemes were not successful, one factor at least caught their attention as seen from the Annual Report and official discussion of education generally. This was that the salary of the primary school teacher was terribly low (Rs.5-7 per month). The result was that it was not possible to attract talent to work as teachers and secondly in many cases teachers took to education only as a secondary employment. To remedy this it was provided that a time scale of increase in teachers salaries be brought into effect.

TABLE 23

No.of Pupils Studying in the English Lower Secondary and Higher Classes in the State

For the year 1912-13

	Brihaminis	Kshatriyas	Vaisyas	Lingayats	Vokkaligars	Panfchamas	Mudaliars	Naidus	Panchalas	Mahratil	Devanga	Banjiga	Ganiga	Satani	Beda	Others	Parsi	Indian Christians	European & Anglo Indians	Mahomedans	Jains	Jetty	Coorgi	Besta	Kuruba	Tailor	Naik	Barber	Mochi	Golla	Total	%age of Brahins to Total	%age of Non Brahmins Total
English Lower Secondary Classes	1,092	27	113	164	94	5	39	27	9	3	18	32	19	13	6	48	—	36	4	116	10	—	4	6	26	2	1	—	—	3	1,916	56.9	42.9
High School Classes	1,682	48	82	127	100	1	39	34	1	1	—	13	—	5	—	60	—	123	12	163	12	—	—	—	5	—	—	1	—	1	2,510	67.5	32.5
College (Arts) Classes	269	4	31	23	10	—	12	10	—	—	1	5	—	—	—	42	1	6	1	5	—	—	2	—	—	-	1	—	—	—	483	62.1	35.2
College (Technical) Classes	529	17	32	56	45	82	23	13	10	5	17	—	—	9	—	96	—	266	13	12	—	3	—	—	18	—	—	—	12	—	1,319	38.6	60.5
Total	3,572	96	258	370	249	88	113	84	20	9	36	10	19	27	6	240	1	431	40	407	22	3	6	6	48	3	1	1	12	4	6,228	57.4	42.0

	Brihaminis	Kshatriyas	Vaisyas	Lingayats	Vokkaligars	Panfchamas	Mudaliars	Naidus	Panchalas	Mahratil	Devanga	Banjiga	Ganiga	Satani	Beda	Others	Parsi	Indian Christians	European & Anglo Indians	Mahomedans	Jains	Jetty	Coorgi	Besta	Kuruba	Tailor	Naik	Barber	Mochi	Golla	Total	%age of Brahins to Total	%age of Non Brahmins Total
For the year 1917-18																																	
English Lower Secondary Classes	2,223	85	246	364	237	23	43	52	18	8	41	46	15	14	2	26	—	95	30	227	36	13	9	7	66	7	1	8	—	1	3,943	56.4	42.9
High School Classes	3,132	111	13	6,120	57	3	39	29	3	10	32	27	—	32	—	64	4	132	5	283	47	5	1	5	3	2	4	3	4	3	4,400	71.2	27.7
College (Arts) Classes	247	11	24	23	1	5	6	—	2	1	—	—	—	—	1	—	4	1	26	5	—	—	—	—	—	—	—	—	—	302	392	68.01	36.22
College (Technical) Classes	829	56	80	99	93	141	45	26	42	14	30	28	9	—	—	330	3	346	51	181	16	—	1	18	4	21	—	15	35	35	2,513	329	46.9
Total	6,431	263	486	698	428	168	132	113	63	34	104	101	24	46	2	421	7	577	87	727	102	18	11	90	73	30	5	24	4	40	11,248	57.2	42.05

Increase or decrease at the end of five years in percentage

Brahmins	On-Brahmine
Minna 2	Plus 05

TABLE 24

Statement of Hostels Attached to the Educations in the State, with the Number of Broaders in Them on the 30th June 1918

Name of Hostels	Brihaminis	Kshatriyas	Vaisyas	Lingayats	Vokkaligars	Panfchamas	Mudaliars	Naidus	Devanga	Satani	Panchalas	Banjiga	Ganiga	Veddy	Nair	Indian Xiani	Europeans and Angl-Indians	Mahomedans	Jains	Kuruba	Beda	Washerman	Barber	Ganlga	Wodda	Total	Total Brahmins	Total Non-Brahmins
Private-Hostels																												
Sarinivasa Mandiram Orphanage	21	-	3	-	-	-	1	1	-	-	-	-	-	-	-	-	-	-	-	-	-	-	-	2	-	28	21	7
Ursu Broading Home, Mysore	81	-	-	-	-	-	-	-	-	-	-	-	-	-	-		-	-	-	-	-	-	-	-	-	81	-	81
Sri Laksminarasimha Dharma Palasala	-	-	-	-	-	-	-	-	-	-	-	-	-	-	-	-	-	-	-	-	-	-	-	30	-	30	-	30
London Mission Boarding Home (Boys),	-	-	-	-	-	-	-	-	-	-	-	-	-	-	-	36	-	-	-	-	-	-	-	-	-	36	-	36
Bangalore																												
Harwicke College, Mysore	-	-	-	-	11	-	-	-	-	-	-	-	-	-	-	70	-	-	-	-	-	-	-	-	-	81	-	81
Wesleyan Mission Orphanage, Tumkur	-	-	-	-	-	-	-	-	-	-	-	-	-	-	-	100	-	-	-	-	-	-	-	-	-	100	-	100
Mission Hotel, Kolar	-	-	-	-	-	9	-	-	-	-	-	-	-	-	-	52	-	-	-	-	-	-	-	-	4	65	-	65
Weslleyan Mission Girls Orphanage, Hassan	-	-	-	-	-	-	-	-	-	-	-	-	-	-	-	102	-	-	-	-	-	-	-	-	-	102	-	102
M.E. Mission Girls Boarding School, Kolar	-	-	-	-	-	-	-	-	-	-	-	-	-	-	-	148	-	-	-	-	-	-	-	-	-	148	-	148
Wasleyan Mission Boarding Home, Bangalore	-	-	-	-	-	-	-	-	-	-	-	-	-	-	-	62	-	-	-	-	-	-	-	-	-	62	-	62
London Mission Girls Home, Bangalore	-	-	-	-	-	-	-	-	-	-	-	-	-	-	-	79	-	-	-	-	-	-	-	-	-	79	-	79
Total	21	81	3	-	11	9	1	1	-	-	-	-	-	-	-	649	-	-	-	-	-	-	-	32	4	812	21	791

Name of Hostels	Brihaminis	Kshatriyas	Vaisyas	Lingayats	Vokkaligars	Panfchamas	Mudaliars	Naidus	Devanga	Satani	Panchalas	Banjiga	Ganiga	Veddy	Nair	Indian Xiani	Europeans and Angl-Indians	Mahomedans	Jains	Kuruba	Beda	Washerman	Barber	Ganlga	Wodda	Total	Total Brahmins	Total Non-Brahmins
Mahomedans Hostels																												
Mohamedan Hostel attached to the Training College, Mysore	-	-	-	-	-	-	-	-	-	-	-	-	-	-	-	-	-	64	-	-	-	-	-	-	-	64	-	64
Central MohamedanAssociation Bangalore	-	-	-	-	-	-	-	-	-	-	-	-	-	-	-	-	-	24	-	-	-	-	-	-	-	24	-	24
Total	-	-	-	-	-	-	-	-	-	-	-	-	-	-	-	-	-	88	-	-	-	-	-	-	-	88	-	88
Special Hostels																												
Hostel for the Deaf and the Blind	12	1	21	1	4	-	-	-	-	-	-	-	-	-	-	-	-	3	-	-	-	-	-	-	-	28	12	11
Agricultural School Hostel, Hebbal	26	1	2	1	-	-	-	-	-	-	-	-	-	1	-	3	-	1	-	-	-	-	-	-	-	35	26	9
Total	38	2	4	2	4	-	-	-	-	-	-	-	-	-	3	-	4	1	-	-	-	-	-	-	58	38	-	90

TABLE 25

Statement of Hostels Attached to the Educational Institutions in the State with the Number of Boarders in Them on the 30th June 1918

Name of Hostels	Brihaminis	Kshatriyas	Vaisyas	Lingayats	Vokkaligars	Panfchamas	Mudaliars	Naidus	Devanga	Satani	Panchalas	Banjiga	Ganiga	Veddy	Nair	Indian Xiani	Europeans and Angl-Indians	Mahomedans	Jains	Kuruba	Beda	Washerman	Barber	Ganlga	Wodda	Total	Total Brahmins	Total Non-Brahmins
Government Hostels																												
District Normal Schools Bangalore	22	-	-	-	-	-	-	-	2	-	-	-	-	-	-	-	-	1	-	-	-	-	-	-	-	25	22	8
Hindus, attached to the training College, Mysore	43	-	-	-	-	-	-	-	-	-	-	-	-	-	-	-	-	-	-	-	-	-	-	-	-	43	43	-
District Normal School, Kolar	16	-	-	1	2	-	-	-	-	-	-	-	-	-	-	-	-	-	-	-	-	-	1	-	-	20	16	4
District Normal School,Tumkur	30	-	2	-	1	-	-	-	-	-	-	-	-	-	-	-	-	-	-	-	-	-	-	-	-	33	30	3
District Normal School,Hassan	26	-	-	4	-	-	-	-	-	-	-	-	-	-	-	-	-	-	-	-	-	-	-	-	-	30	26	4
District Normal School Shimoga	16	-	-	-	-	-	-	-	-	1	1	1	-	-	-	1	-	-	-	-	-	1	1	-	-	22	16	10
District Normal School, Chitradurga	16	-	-	-	1	-	-	1	3	-	1	-	-	-	1	-	-	-	-	-	-	-	-	-	-	26	16	10
District Normal School,attached to Govt. High School, Channapatna	24	-	-	-	2	-	1	-	-	-	-	1	-	-	-	-	-	-	-	-	-	-	-	-	-	28	24	4
Government High Schol, Kolar	14	-	-	-	-	-	1	3	-	-	-	-	1	-	-	-	-	-	-	-	-	-	-	-	-	19	14	5
Government High School, Chikballapur	10	1	-	-	3	-	-	-	-	-	-	-	-	-	-	-	-	-	-	-	-	-	-	-	-	14	10	4
Government High School, Tumkur	54	-	1	-	3	-	1	1	-	-	-	-	-	-	1	-	-	-	-	-	-	-	-	-	-	61	54	7
Government High School, Hasan	15	-	-	-	2	-	-	-	-	-	-	-	-	-	-	-	-	-	-	-	-	-	-	-	-	17	15	2
Government High Schol, Chikmagalur	8	-	-	-	3	-	-	-	-	-	-	-	-	-	-	-	-	-	1	-	-	-	-	-	12	8	4	
Government High School, Shimoga	37	2	-	-	2	-	-	-	-	-	-	-	-	-	-	-	-	-	-	-	-	-	-	-	-	41	37	4

Name of Hostels	Brihaminis	Kshatriyas	Vaisyas	Lingayats	Vokkaligars	Panfchamas	Mudaliars	Naidus	Devanga	Satani	Panchalas	Banjiga	Ganiga	Veddy	Nair	Indian Xiani	Europeans and Angl-Indians	Mahomedans	Jains	Kuruba	Beda	Washerman	Barber	Ganlga	Wodda	Total	Total Brahmins	Total Non-Brahmins
Government High School, Chitradurga	8	-	-	-	-	-	-	-	4	-	-	-	-	2	2	-	-	-	-	1	-	-	-	-	-	17	8	2
Government High School, Mysore	22	-	-	-	-	-	-	-	-	-	-	-	-	-	-	-	-	-	-	-	-	-	-	-	-	22	22	-
Government High School, Engineering School, Mysore	22	-	1	-	1	-	-	-	-	-	-	-	-	-	-	-	-	-	-	-	-	-	-	-	-	26	22	4
Maharani's College	19	1	2	1	2	-	-	-	-	-	-	-	-	-	1	5	-	-	-	-	-	-	-	-	-	31	19	12
Women's Home, Mysore, Hostel Mysore	33	-	1	-	-	-	-	-	-	-	-	-	-	-	-	-	-	-	-	-	-	-	-	-	-	35	33	2
Total	435	4	7	6	23	-	3	6	9	1	2	2	1	2	5	6	-	1	1	5	-	1	2	-	-	522	435	87

TABLE 26

Statement Showing the Number of Freeships Granted to Pupils of the Different Communities in the English Lower Secondary and Higher Classes During 1915-16, 1916-16 and 1917-18

Number of Freeships give in	Brihaminis	Kshatriyas	Vaisyas	Lingayats	Vokkaligars	Panfchamas	Mudaliars	Naidus	Panchalas	Mahratil	Devanga	Banjiga	Ganiga	Satani	Beda	Others	Parsi	Indian Christians	European & Anglo Indians	Mahomedans	Jains	Jetty	Coorgi	Besta	Kuruba	Tailor	Naik	Barber	Mochi	Golla	Total	%age of Brahins to Total	%age of Non Brahmins Total
Entrance Class																																	
1915-16	-	-	-	-	-	-	-	-	-	-	-	-	-	-	-	-	-	-	-	-	-	-	-	-	-	-	-	-	-	-			
1916-17	88	-	10	18	4	-	4	3	-	-	-	1	-	-	-	-	-	-	-	-	-	8	-	-	-	-	-	-	-	-	-	-	136
1917-18	97	4	14	17	18	-	6	7	-	-	-	-	-	-	-	-	-	-	-	-	-	9	-	4	-	-	-	-	-	-	-	-	166
High School																																	
1915-16	321	9	6	19	21	-	8	5	1	1	1	-	-	-	-	-	-	-	1	-	-	44	-	6	-	-	-	-	-	-	-	2	446
1916-17	388	22	11	31	32	-	13	12	3	-	-	-	1	2	1	-	-	-	1	-	-	66	-	9	-	-	-	-	-	-	-	-	597
1917-18	392	22	20	25	39	-	19	12	-	2	-	-	3	1	-	5	2	1	-	1	1	55	-	15	-	-	-	-	-	-	-	1	612
English Lower Secondary Classses																																	
1915-16	297	14	18	32	35	1	4	5	2	-	5	2	6	-	-	-	-	-	22	-	-	48	-	15	1	-	1	-	-	-	-	-	518
1916-17	343	9	13	49	25	213	8	1	3	-	6	4	2	-	-	-	4	-	14	1	1	46	1	16	-	2	-	-	1	1	1	12	578
1917-18	459	17	17	42	98	14	17	3	16	3	4	3	4	1	-	-	3	-	20	1	1	64	8	1	-	2	2	2	-	4	2	1	813
Technical Schools																																	
1915-16	1	-	-	-	-	-	-	-	-	-	-	-	-	-	-	-	-	-	-	-	-	-	-	-	-	-	-	-	-	-	-	-	1
1916-17	1	-	-	-	-	-	-	-	-	-	-	-	-	-	-	-	-	-	-	-	-	-	-	-	-	-	-	-	-	-	-	-	1
1917-18	48	1	1	-	-	-	2	1	-	-	-	-	-	-	-	-	-	-	1	-	-	4	-	-	-	-	-	-	-	-	-	-	58

TABLE 27

Statement Showing the Number of Scholarship Granted Pupils of the Different Communities in the State Studying in the English Lower Secondary and Eigher Classes During 1915-16, 1916-17 and 1917-18

	Brihaminis	Kshatriyas	Vaisyas	Lingayats	Vokkaligars	Panfchamas	Mudaliars	Naidus	Pallegara	Telugu Banajiga	Satani	Bedas	Besta	Barber	Indian Christians	Europeans and Anglo-Indians	Mahomedans	Jains	Total
University Entrance Class																			
1915-16	-	-	-	-	-	-	-	-	-	-	-	-	-	-	-	-	-	-	-
1916-17	5	1	-		-	-	-	-	-	-	-	-	-		1	1	3		8
1917-18	6	3	2	23	6	1	3	7	-	-	-	-	-	-	3	-	11	4	76
High Schools																			
1915-16	12	-	-	1	-	-	-	-	3	-	-	-	-	-	-	1	12	1	30
1916-17	13	-	-	1	2	-	-	-	3	-	-	-		-	2	2	22	-	45
1917-18	24	10	6	20	20	-	2	3	3	8	4	6	3	2	4	2	57	8	260
English Secondary Class																			
1915-16	16	1	-	4	2	-	-	-	2	1	-	1	-	-	-	-	3	-	35
1916-17	17	3	11	29	40	26	3	4	1	1	-	40	41	2	8	-	15	1	244
1917-18	18	18	14	82	56	42	8	13	-	37	-	122	120	3	13	-	48	2	595

TABLE 28

StatementOf appopintment held by the different communities in the state service on 30th June 1916, 30th June 1917 and 30th June 1918

Appointment										Other Hindus, each caste to be seperately mentioned																Other Communities, if any, each to be separ-ately mentioned						
		Brihaminis	Kshatriyas	Vaisyas	Lingayats	Vokkaligars	Panfchamas	Mudaliars	Naidus	Maharatta	Goldsmiths	Jetties	Naikers	Satanis	Banajigars	Gollars	Kurubara	Pillaya	Tailors	Chetties	Other minor divisions	Indian Christians	European & Anglo Indians	Mahomedans	Jains	Malayalis	Parsis	Coorgies	Bengalis	Gujarathis	Other Communities	Total
Appointments carrying a pay of less than Rs.25 per monsem (Superior) service only	1916	4,903	117	39	340	222	31	79	80	62	4	3	8	26	70	18	37	8	4	-	251	255	10	744	24	5	-	2	-	-	3	-
	1917	5,171	124	35	393	241	32	39	87	88	5	10	12	29	79	12	62	8	7	2	289	232	8	779	32	7	7	2	5	-	6	-
	1918	5,607	148	41	412	258	59	74	86	57	4	12	12	29	89	18	44	11	10	2	322	257	11	303	34	7	1	3	-	-	-	-
Appointments carrying a salary from Rs. 25 to Rs. 50	1916	2,282	43	30	43	40	6	196	94	11	1	1	2	2	5	4	3	18	-	1	31	71	21	150	10	1	-	3		-	-	-
	1917	2,484	42	27	52	46	7	202	100	9	3	3	3	2	4	4	2	18	-	1	40	72	19	171	10	3	-	5	-	-	1	-
	1918	14	10	17	18	-	66	36	1	1	1	-	1	3	-	2	4	-	3	14	36	41	49	3	-	2	1	-	-	3	-	
	1916	882	16	10	25	18	-	63	36	4	-	-	-	-	2	-	2	5	-	1	12	45	41	65	1	-	2	1	1	-	-	-
Do Rs. 250	1917	106	2	1	4	2	-	5	3	-	-	-	-	-	-	-	-	3	-	-	4	9	6	9	1	-	1	2	-	-	-	-
to 450	1918	122	2	-	2	2	-	4	2	-	-	-	-	-	-	-	-	1	-	-	6	7	8	5	-	-	1	1	-	-	1	-
	1918	150	4	-	5	3	-	5	4	-	-	-	-	-	1	-	-	1	1	-	2	5	17	13	-	-	1	1	-	-	1	-
Do Rs. 450	1916	40	4	-	2	-	-	-	-	-	-	-	-	-	-	-	-	-	-	-	2	5	7	1	-	1	-	1	1	-	1	-
to 800	1917	39	3	-	2	-	-	1	-	-	-	-	-	-	-	-	-	-	-	-	2	4	5	-	1	1	3	2	2	-	1	-
	1918	49	1	1	2	-	-	1	2	-	-	-	-	-	-	-	-	-	-	-	1	5	7	-	1	-	3	5	2	-	1	-
Do Rs. 800 and upwards	1916	32	1	-	-	1	-	1	-	-	-	-	-	-	-	-	-	-	-	-	-	3	17	1	-	-	1	-	1	-	-	-

Appointment		Brihaminis	Kshatriyas	Vaisyas	Lingayats	Vokkaligars	Panchamas	Mudaliars	Naidus	Maharatta	Goldsmiths	Jetties	Naikers	Satanis	Banajigars	Gollars	Kurubara	Pillaya	Tailors	Chetties	Other minor divisions	Indian Christians	European & Anglo Indians	Mahomedans	Jains	Malayalis	Parsis	Coorgies	Bengalis	Gujarathis	Other Communities	Total
										Other Hindus, each caste to be seperately mentioned																Other Communities, if any, each to be separ-ately mentioned						
	1917	35	2	-	-	1	-	2	-	-	-	-	-	-	-	-	-	-	-	-	-	2	15	2	-	1	1	-	-	-	-	-
	1918	41	4	-	-	1	-	1	-	-	-	-	-	-	-	-	-	-	-	-	1	5	17	3	-	-	1	-	1	-	-	-
	1916	8,286	184	80	411	288	37	380	224	76	6	5	11	27	79	22	41	37	7	8	299	394	121	955	37	8	5	9	2	2	6	12,055
Total	1917	8,911	188	75	477	311	39	382	232	78	9	14	15	32	88	17	66	33	8	6	364	364	143	10,23	46	13	8	11	2	2	12	212,958
	1918	9,712	220	76	504	338	67	377	242	84	9	8	15	34	101	15	48	38	11	5	384	395	156	1078	44	11	7	14	4	1	7	13,946

TABLE 29

Statement of Employees in the Government Service Compared with Total Population and the Literature among Them

Caste or Race Percentage	Total population	Literate population	Literate in English	Number attending School (Lower Secondary and Higher Classes)	Total in Govt. Service (Superior)	No. of Rs. 100 and below	N0. on Rs. 100 to Rs. 250	Number above Rs. 250	Percentage of 3 to 2	Percentage of 4 to 2	Percentage of 6 to 2
1	2	3	4	5	6	7	8	9	10	11	12
HINDU											
Brahmin	193,137	80,409	15,455	6,481	9,712	9.110	362	240	41.63	8	.5
Kshatriya	36,894	6,031	638	263	220	206	5	9	16,34	1.7	.6
Vakkaliga	1,328,237	42,206	737	426	338	330	4	4	3.17	06	.02
Lingayal	728,571	66,665	804	698	504	487	10	7	9,15	1	.07
Mudaliar Other Hindus not specially backward,	11,871	3,217	799	122	377	351	19	7	27.1	6	3.1
Specially backward or Depressed	627.891	64,059	1,499	1,001	1,001	954	16	31	5.15	2	.16
Classes	2,447,636	31,467	636	107	.165	165	-	-	2.6	07	.007
Mahomedans	291,708	34,831	1,307	727	1,078	1,045	17	16	11.9	.5	.4
Indian Christians	34,201	7,820	2.431	577	395	373	7	15	22.8	7.1	1.2
Europeans andAnglo Indians	5,213	4,109	3,987	87	156	71	44	41	80.5	76	3
Total	5,703,359	340,904	29,190	11.240	13,946	13,092	484	370	5.9	.5	.24

In 1918 C.R.Reddy was appointed as Inspector General of Education. The next year, under his directions the Government came out with a comprehensive document on education.

The education memorandum was prepared by C.R.Reddy after taking into consideration the opinions of educational institutions the Assembly the Economic Conference and several leading public men. This document was brought into effect in May 1921.

According to the Memorandum every grade of education was separate and unconnected with the next or higher grade. This was the principal defect. Education had to be considered as one comprehensive unity and all development had to take peace keeping this linkage in view according in the Memorandum. Further the Memo observed that there was need uniformity in Schools.

Regarding Primary Schools the Memo suggested that there should be

Primary school for every 600-population

Primary school for every 2.9 sq miles of areas.

Primary school for every 60 pupils in age of 7-10 years.

The State's population was 6 million and the Memo wanted 10000 schools in a total period of 5 years from the date. Further the following teacher pupil ratio was suggested:-

Enrolment less than 30 in 4 standard 1 teacher

-do-	30 to 60 in 4 standards = 2 teachers
-do-	60 to 90 in 4 standards = 3 teachers
-do-	90 to 120 in 4 standards = 4 teachers

The minimum pay of teachers was fixed at the Rs. 12 per month while the total pay would be Rs. 20 including allowances.

Regarding middle schools this document recommended that they should be entirely unilanguage with English because a pass in English language was expected for entry into High Schools. Hence Vernacular Middle Schools were to be abolished. English was to be introduced as a second language in Middle schools. The number of Middle Schools was to be increased to 600 in 5 years. The Memo did not recommend any radical changes in High Schools.

After 1921 the government went on operating the recommendations of the Education Memorandum. There were a variety of problems and these were solved to the extent possible. But after the departure of C.R. Reddy from Mysore in 1922, both the backward Class Movement and the educational development felt the lack of dynamism further, after 1918 the state faced financial problems and this told heavily on the educational development.

Mysore Elementary Education Regulation—1930

In the history of Elementary Education in Mysore state, the year 1930 constitutes a landmark. But the important developments of that year can be properly understood only in the context of nothing the historical developments in the field of local self-governing institutions in the state.

The history of modern local self governing institutions in Mysore state go back to the year 1872, when the Local Fund rules were brought into forced. Under these rules district Fund Boards were constituted to administer, 76% of certain local cesses that were collected. The remaining 24% was constituted as Village School Fund and was administered by the state government for educational purposes.

After 1872 reforms in local self government came in 1902, 1918 and 1926. Under these reforms, local bodies were given powers to maintain, supervise and administer Primary Schools in the respective areas under their jurisdiction. Meanwhile in 1919 came the Montfored Committee recommendations. According to this Committee local bodies needed strengthening and particularly it was recommended that they be given powers of a wide nature regarding nation building subjects. Education at the primary level was one of the important aspects of nation building.

Beginning from 1925-26 a debate ensued in the official circles in Mysore regarding the need for reforming local bodies in the state. While at one stage this debate led to the passing of statutes reforming the constitution of local bodies and enlarging their powers and functions in 1930, the state brought into effect the Mysore Elementary Education Regulation. This statute was seriously debated both in the Representative Assembly and the Legislative Council. The original bill was modified and passed.

The purpose of this Act was the progressive expansion of elementary Education and the Investment of local authorities with powers for control of Elementary education and a definition of the same.

According to this Act, Municipal Councils, District Boards and Municipalities were Constituted as Local Education Authorities.

1. The Local Education Authorities were responsible for the consolidation expansion and development of Elementary Education.
2. All Primary Schools were to be subject to local. Education Authorities. The LEA was to administer

grants and all state grants to education were transferred to LEA.

3. The LEA was to employ, teachers but in case of necessity teachers could appeal to Government.
4. The pay of teachers at time of take over was not to be altered by LEA.
5. Fees were not to be levied in Primary Schools by LEA.
6. The LEA was to conform to regulations issued by Government regarding courses of study, syllabus building standards, standards of teachers, their qualifications, hours of school, inspection and inspection norms of children. If LEA failed to conform, to Government regulations grants given to it would be deducted.
7. For purposes of finance, the LEA, could levy local cess at rates fixed by Government, could raise loans and could collect subscription and donations. The LEA had to submit its annual budget and statements of income, expenditure to Government.
8. The LEA had to constitute a board for schools in the area under its jurisdiction. These Boards had to function under supervision and control of the LEA.
9. Within 1 year the LEA had to prepare plans for expansion of Primary Education for a 10 years period. So that there was atleast one school in every village panchayat area.
10. Under this statute all children in ages 6-12 years were to compulsorily attend school except.
    a. If there was no recognized school within one mile from place of residence.
    b. In case of sickness, infirmity

c. In case a child was receiving some other form of suitable instruction or was Exempted by proper authority

11. Children in school age were exempted from religious instruction classes if parents wished.
12. Children in school age were not to be employed during school hours.
13. Parents who responsible for going against these rules could be fined Rs.2/- by a magistrate after warning notice. If they did not comply they could be fined Rs.10/- Persons who employed children's in school age knowingly could be fined Rs. 20/-

Very quickly it became clear that the programme of educational expansion especially at the Primary stage contemplated path under the 1931 Statute was not likely to be realized. In 1933, the Government appointed a committee to consider the question of reorganization of education at all levels below the University stage. This committee submitted its report in 1936. According to this Report there should be three grades of schools as

1. Primary school	-	6 years duration
2. Middle School	-	3 years duration
3. High School	-	3 years duration

As the Middle and High School levels there were to be general and vocational instruction according to choice by pupil guided by parents. This report also recommended the conduct of an Educational survey which was carried out in 1938. This Survey clearly brought out the fact that the 1931 statute had failed. Hence after considerable debate in the Assembly and Council the Government withdrew the 1931 law and brought into force the Mysore Elementary Education Act of 1941.

5

Educational Administration and Controlling Agencies in Mysore Princely State

One of the important aspects of the modern education system is the controlling agency. As education has become a part of state activity, control and direction of activity of educational institutions has become a significant area of state activity. Control and direction of educational activity is aimed to ensure uniformity in standards of work and activity, to direct check and correct educational activity and most significantly to see that the benefits of education are available to people at large. In fact if the history of education could be studied from the point of view of cultural hegemony, it is through the controlling agency system that this hegemony is sought to the established. However such a study is beyond the scope of the present essay.

While the state or government through its Department of public Instruction or Education directly controls and directs the educational activity, there are other agencies, bodies and for a which exert influence and pressure on state direction of educational activity. Fore example the public press is a potent for .e and a powerful influence. In Princely Mysore, the ne' vspaper press did take note of educational activity. But, the sources for such a study are stray and hence it is not attempted here. Secondly, in Mysore state there were the Mysore Representative Assembly and the Mysore Legislative Council, the former started in 1881 and the latter started in 1907. While these two bodies were established with a view only to ventilate public grievances from about the 1820s they exerted influences on state policy.

Department of Public Instruction 1857 to 1900

Until 1857, the schools that existed in Mysore State were not controlled by the state authority the Department of Public Instruction and an Inspectorate under it were formed in keeping with the Halifax Dispatch. The Department of Public Instruction was to function under the supervision of the Judicial Commissioner of the State. This department was to consist of:

1) A Director of Public Instruction
2) Two Inspectors of Schools
3) Four Deputy Inspectors of School (one for each Division)
4) Twenty four Sub-Deputy Inspectors of Schools one for every four taluks.

In 1863, the Department of Public, Instruction was separated from the office of Judicial Commissioner. But between 1857-1867 the entire state was under overall supervision of one Inspector only. That year when the second inspector was appointed the state was divided into 2 circles.

Circle I : Districts of Bangalore, Kolar, Mysore, Hassan

Circle II: Districts of Shimoga, Kadur, Chitradurga and Tumkur

In 1868 the inspectorate was reorganized as under : -

1) Director of Public Instruction

2) Two Circle Inspectors of Schools
3) One Deputy Inspector of Schools
4) Eight Sub - deputy Inspector of Schools for the districts.

The Sub - deputy Inspectors were to visit schools in their districts thrice a year and make a qualitative report of the institutions in very general terms on the basis of attendance, of teachers and pupils and their respective progress.

The Inspectorate consisting of Circle Inspectors and Sub Deputy Inspectors not only inspected schools but conducted examination also where the fitness or otherwise of students selectively presented was decided till 1871 this convocation was conducted at the district level and from that year at the taluk level. This arrangement more or less continued till 1900, though there were administrative changes and increases in staff in 1872, 1875, 1879, 1881 and 1893.

In addition to examinations and progress reports for pupils and their teachers, the Inspectors had to account for slack attendance and other problems faced by schools. The report of 1867 - 68 gives the following interesting details regarding a school in Siddlaghatta – " the disadvantageous situation of the school as before explained continues to be a chief matter of complaint. Not only is it outside the town but it is on the wrong side in a quarter which is never visited by the people. I may here mention that it is a spot associated with a peculiar superstition, for I am informed that when the people are attacked by severe fever or other sickness of a dangerous character, they make small idols of clay which after the performance of, ceremonies imagined to the effacatious, in such cases they bring out and cast away in the tope adjoining the school. Thus as they suppose ridding themselves of the noxious infection which by a further effort of the imagination may be considered naturally to adhere to the region. This together with the unprotected nature of the place which renders little children to be robbed of their ornaments an instance having occurred only a few days ago makes parents unwilling to risk sending their boys there. The master has therefore to appoint a place of rendezvous within the town where all the pupils assemble that they may go to the school in a body accompanied by him". There are also numerous references how many schools were not regularly inspected because of lack of time for the Inspecting staff had to constantly be on the move.

Hobli School Panchayats

Under the Hobli School scheme of 1868, each school was to be immediately supervised by a panchayat consisting of village elders selected by the Deputy Commissioner on the recommendations of the Amuldar. Such panchayats were formed in a few schools only and there is no information as to how they worked. From the information furnished in the able below it is clear that they would have had general supervision responsibilities only as leading citizens of the villages.

TABLE 30

Panchayats in the Hobli Schools

District	*Village*	*Panchayat*
Kolar	Ambajidurga	Shanbhog Naranappa gowda
		Yerrappa Reddi Rachappa Chetty
	Betamangala	Shanbhog Krishnappa, Peddapalli
		Sinappa, Thimme Gowda
		Shanbhog Bhimraya Dontimata
		Srinivasa Chetty Ganigara
		Venkatanaranapp
		Shanbhog Gumasta Surappa,
		Bashi Reddi.

District	*Village*	*Panchayat*
	Avati	Shanbhog Venkatarayappa Thimmaraya Gowda, Carpenter Venkatappa
	Nandi	Shanbhog subbia Chetty, Appia, Pensioner salarkhan
	Hampasandra	Shanbhog Subbanna, Marri Nanjundappa, Mata Venkataramania
	Devarayasandra	Gowda Ananthia Yejaman Pattabhiramaia Shanbhog subbanna Muneshwaria Naranappa, Margha Subbia Bhatta
	Sugaturu	Shanbhog Balappa Jamindar Kodandappa, Ryot Muniappa
	Mudawadi	Gowda Seshagiri raò Shanbhog Seenappa, Chetty Basanna
	Hulidenahalli	Rangegowda, Shanbhog Nagappa Kumbara Appanna
	Lakkuru	Adike Govindappa, Attibele Naranappa.
	Kudaganuru	Bacha Chetty, Ryot Viris Nilkantaraya
	Yeleduru	Shanbhog Bhogappa, Yeldeduru Narain Rays, Nanjegowda
	Nambihalli	Shanbhog Doddalingappa Sitaramia, Thell Annia Setty rangia
Mysore	Chilkalnerpu	Shanbhog Rayappa, Malapatti Reddanna Adappa
Mysore	Muttegere	Gurusiddia, Maregowda, Kadegowda,
	Mudagandur	Venkataramana Dasashetty Honnachalli Cheni Gowda
	Basaralu	Chikkachetty, Badra Chetty Dase Gowda

District	Village	Panchayat
Chikmagalur	Muttavara	Shanbhog Aswathia Patil Chennegowda
	Hirimagaluru	Potail cheluvia Shanghog Venkatappa
	Kalasapura	Narayanappa, Shanbhog Sankarappa
	Malluru	Potail Doddegowda Shanbhog Subbarao
	Lakki	Potail Malle Gowda Shanbhog Thimmanna
	Narayanapura	Potail Basave gowda, Shanbhog Venkataramania

Village School Committees

Addressing the Representative Assembly in 1893 Seshadri Iyar referred to the urgent need to strengthen local governing institutions particularly in the matter of education. He further said that School Committees were to be formed to supervise the working of schools at the village level. These village school committees were to consist of 3 - 5 intelligent villagers preferably those who had children, selected by the Deputy Commissioners on the recommendations of the Amildars. Sannads were issued to the members according to which they were to visit schools, enforce and check on attendance of teachers, see to the maintenance of cleanliness in the school premises check the regularly of school work, note and bring to the notice of higher auothritities any irregularities and see to the maintenance of maps furniture and etc. There is no data as to how many such committees were formed nor as to how they actually worked, their actual composition and so on. They continued in existence till practically the end of the period of this study. Till about the 1920s the Government and the department seem to be happy about these committees as seen from the reports from which the two extracts below have been chosen. In 1902 - 03, the report observes, most of the Village School Committees have been reconstituted with a view to increase the strength of the non - Brahmin element on them. The committees as a rule have given help in keeping up attendance enforcing discipline and seeing that the teacher is not absent without leave and is attentive to his work. They take however little interest in the question of providing accommodation for schools which they think is the duty of the Government to provide. Similarly in 1907 – the report observes" most of the village school committees are reported to have taken a fair amount of interest in the welfare of their schools. Many of them co - operated with the inspecting officers in checking the unauthorized absence of school masters and in attending to the regular maintenance of school registers and other records as well as to the discipline of the schools. They also exercised vigilance over the attendance of pupils and the work of the teachers and reported drawbacks to the Inspecting Officers and gave useful suggestions for the improvement of the schools. The members of school committees as rule were present at the inspection of their schools. Few Committees however took active steps either to provide suitable new buildings or to repair and improve the existing ones. This neglect is chiefly due to the poverty of the villagers and insufficient appreciation of the benefits of education."

In 1918 however, the report gives a different picture, altogether when it observes that these Committees are ineffective because the members are illiterate.

Visits of Revenue Officiers

In 1894, Government issued an order to the effect that revenue officers of the Government should visit periodically the schools in the areas under their jurisdiction and areas oversee their working generally. Every Report of the Department till the end of this period covered by this study refers to these visits but nothing is known about the results of these visits. It is obvious from the Reports that the Department of Public Instruction often did not come out with realistic observations about the usefulness of the work of these Revenue Officers. Every Report gives the number of visits and sometimes there are references indicating reluctance on the part of the officers to do such work. Below are two samples of data about such visit from the Reports of 1906 and 1929.

Development in Inspectorate (1900 - 1940)

Between 1900 and 1940 the Department of Public Instruction was reorganized from time to time in 1906, 1921, 1927 and 1941. These changes were respectively as follows.

In 1906 – 07 after reorganization the Department consisted of : Inspector General of Education Two Circle Inspectors for the 2 circles (East and West) Deputy Inspectors for the 8 Districts One Deputy Inspector for Hindustan (Urdu) schools. Assistant Deputy Inspectors for the 13 Ranges.

Prior to 1921 in, 1915, 20 Educational Supervisors were appointed to relieve the Deputy Inspectors of their work load. But C.R.Reddy was doubtful of their utility in inspection work. Consequently these posts were abolished by Government in 1921, and the numbers of Assistant Deputy Inspectors was increased to 60.

In 1927, 3 Provincial Inspectors, an Inspectresses and 5 Assistant Inspectresses for Girls Schools, 3 District Inspectors, 4 Assistant Inspectors and 2 Assistant Inspectresses for Muslim Schools were appointed.

Later in 1941, the Entire Primary Education System was separately placed under charge of a Deputy Director Elementary Education, with separate Education officers one for each District these were the major changes in the Inspectorate between 1900 - 1941.

TABLE 31

No. of Visits

	Kannada and Anglo - Kannada Schools									
Officers	*Bangalore*	*Kolar*	*Tumkur*	*Mysore*	*Chitradurg*	*Shimoga*	*Hassan*	*Kadur*	*Hindustani*	*Total*
Deputy Commissioners	4	12	1	1	18	5	5	7	5	58
Senior Assistant Commissioner	—	17	—	—	—	—	—	—	—	17
Assistant Commissioners	44	32	21	21	16	14	16	7	9	180
Amildars and Deputy Amildars	26	18	44	29	34	20	15	16	5	207
Other Government Officers	27	19	25	22	26	2	8	16	16	161
Total	101	98	91	72	94	41	45	46	35	623

TABLE 32

No. of Visits

Name of officers	*Bangalore*	*Kolar*	*Tumkur*	*Mysore*	*Hassan*	*Kadur*	*Shimoga*	*Chitradurg*	*Total*
1. Revenue Commissioner	—	—	—	—	—	2	2	—	4
2. Deputy Commissioner	7	18	8	24	6	8	13	25	109
3. Sub-Divisional Officers or Assistant Commissioner	19	12	18	31	26	8	65	26	205
4. Amildars and Deputy Amildars	70	—	86	67	30	15	95	76	439
5. Others	46	19	60	81	79	33	98	52	468
Total	142	49	172	203	141	66	273	179	1225

After the first reorganization in 1906 the Report in 1907, observes that the inspecting officers were able to pay greater attention to teaching methods gives model lessons and generally improve the tone and discipline of schools. But three years later in 1910, the Department complained that the staff for inspection work was not sufficient for the quantum of work was large and officers worked under pressure. Finally this Report observed very realistically that the problem was because education in Mysore was a huge state enterprise.

After 1900 the nature of inspection also under went many changes which while impercitibile superficially, are indicative of the changing face of inspection as such, In 1920 for example, one circle Inspector "took prompt action to remedy the defects noticed during his inspection, introduced improvements in methods of teaching scrutinized Time Tables and remodeled exercise books"

In 1930, one Assistant Inspectress in Tumkur district held gatherings of "ladies to popularize girls education". Similarly in 1932 Inspecting Officers organized teachers Conferences. While during the 1920s and 1930s, Inspecting Officers are known to have organized Lectures for the benefit of teachers.

In spite of all such efforts as the Inspection report of 1920 observes. "Taking the Inspectorate as a whole, whatever good work it has been able to do, and it has done much good work, one thing may be safely said, viz., that the following up of the inspection is little in evidence. It seems as though an Inspectors duty is considered to have been discharged when amongst other things he discovers faults in schools and teachers and points them out to the persons concerned; and perhaps also when a report is received on "action taken" What he could have rectified when he was on the spot, and what exactly is the action taken to rectify things and suitability of that action to achieve the desired result and whether the desired results are achieved or not are matters which escape his active attention. Circulars of instructions to remedy this defect have been issued and I am hopeful that those circulars will bear the expected results."

Further in many years, reports indicate that many schools were not inspected. The reasons for this were several but mainly, it was due to the fact that an inspecting officer had to be constantly on tour, some times for as much as 200 days in a year. This was obviously strenuous and naturally many schools were not inspected. Secondly as evidenced from several reports, the officers were often slack in their work.

School Boards Under Lea (1931)

As already noticed these Boards were constituted under the Local Education Authorities as per the statute of 1931. These Boards were to conduct one meeting every month to discuss issues related to their schools and find solutions. Available data between 1932 and 1938 indicates that many school Boards conducted additional meetings. Several, Boards did not conduct even one meeting a month. Further as seen from the Reports they are supposed to have discussed a very large number of subjects in each meeting making it clear that the discussion itself was very superficial often.

Role of Representative Assembly and Legislative Council

The Mysore representative Assembly was established in 1881 with the purpose of informing the people of the achievements of the government during the previous year and also the programmes for the next year. Till 1923 this body did not have any statutory basis and further it was not armed with powers to direct or control the government. Naturally the members did not question governmental policy nor did they criticize the same. They usually asked questions or more properly made only representations on various subjects. On the question of Primary and Secondary Education the member of MRA raised number of brief questions and made representations. Answers to the questions were very brief and there is no indication of the government being influenced. Below we gave a list of some subjects raised in the MRA for several years.

Gradually the number of issues raised relating to education increased after 1920. In 1913 when passing the Compulsory Elementary Education regulation, the debate was very brief and there was nothing materially significant. In 1924 June several members made observations on the difficulties in working the Compulsory Education Regulations. It is very significant that the members of the Assembly fully supported the 1931 law relating to transfer of responsibility for primary education to local bodies. Again it should be understood that in many sessions the subject of education was not at all raised. After 1924, when the Assembly gained the power to discuss the budget there were cut motions tagged to education also.

The Mysore Legislative Council was founded in 1907 with the purpose of giving the popular representatives a small measure of control over legislative matters through the final authority rested with the maharaja and the paramount power. The Legislative council like the Assembly discussed a variety of subjects connected generally with legislations that had been brought into effect and education was one such. But since the debates of the Legislative Council till 1926 are not available it is impossible to assess its work.

When the 1931 statute relating to Local Control on Primary Education was brought in the Council very heartily approved of it after lengthy discussions. These discussions generally related to the question whether the District Boards in the state had the necessary capacity for regulating education for at that time they were not very active. After 1931 till 1941, Education was briefly referred in the council especially during the discussions of the budget and they bear comparison with discussions in the Assembly.

6

Financing of Education in Mysore Princely State

One of the important aspects of modern education is educational finance. The importance of finance arises from the fact, that unlike in the pre-modern periods, education is a charge on state expenditure. Naturally, a study of the financial aspects of educational development would indicate the priorities of state expenditure and in turn the attitude of the modern state regarding spending on education.

The colonial power entered Mysore State in 1799. That very year, the Governor General instructed the British Resident in Mysore to watch and indirectly manage the revenues of Mysore State so that, there was no lapse in the effective realisation of the subsidy due to the East India Company under the conditions of the Subsidiary Treaty.

From 1799 to 1831 the state was indirectly under the control of the East India Company. When in 1831, the company took over the administration after the Nagar revolt the state came under British administration. But between 1831 and 1854, the state did not spend any thing on education at all. Whatever schools were started during this period were financed by the Christian missions or Muslim or Hindu religious institutions entirely. The Rajah's school was financed by the Maharaja from his personal funds.

Expenditure of Education 1854-1900

Hard date on the amounts disbursed on Primary and Secondary education between 1854 and 1900 is not available in the sources at our disposal. However, the available data is indicative of the fact that amount was very meager. The data is presented in two parts, the first covering the period 1854-1858 and second, covering the period from 1866 to 1900. There are breaks in the data but these were not avoidable. The figures for 1880 could be taken as valid for the period till 1900 because the variation is very small and is hence not very relevant.

Local Funds and Education

As already noted Local Fund Boards were created in

TABLE 33

Expenditure Towards Education

Year	*Head of Expenditure*	*Amount Rs. As. Ps*
1854-55	Govt. Engineering Education Institution and Provincial schools	9000.0.0
	Slates	13.0.0
1855-56	Govt. Engineering Educational Institution and Provincial schools	14200.0.0
	Books	339.0.0
1856-57	Govt. Engineering Educational Institution and Provincial schools	14050.0.0
1857-58	Director of Public Instruction and	9900.0.0
	Inspector of Schools-Establishment	5513.0.0
	Govt. Engineering Educational Institution and Provincial Schools	19644.0.0
	Books	283.0.0

TABLE 34

Financial Allocation for Education

Years	*Head*	*Total* *Rs. As. Ps.*
1866-67	Education Establishment	91483.0.0
	Education	28720.0.0
1867-68	Education	155064.0.0
1868-69	Education	181280.0.0
1873-74	Education	235631.0.0
1874-75	Education	206009.0.0
1876-77	Education	241175.0.0
1877-78	Education	228679.0.0
1878-79	Education	226652.0.0
1879-80	Education	214407.0.0

Local Funds and Education

As already noted Local Fund Boards were created in Mysore state in 1872. But these bodies did not have finances, "rather the Government created a body to manage certain financial sources". These Boards were to use 76% of local cessess on land revenue which included taxes on houses, shops, carts looms etc. for development works. The board had to use 24% of these revenues exclusively for education within the taluk. In later years, while the financial sources of Local Boards were increased they continued to contribute 24% of their revenues for educational development. This development related almost entirely to education at the Primary and Secondary stages.

Between 1872 and 1900 the Local Boards in the state contributed between 18% to 20% of the total annual expenditure on education for the entire state. Later in 1916-17 the contribution was 18% ; in 1917-18 19%, in 1918-19 18%, in 1919-20 19%, in 1920-21 23% and in 1921-22 23% of the total expenditure on education. Between 1923 and 1940 also the local bodies contributed significantly. But while at the District and Taluk levels after 1902, local bodies were functioning very successfully, at the level of Village Panchayats which were created in 1918 the people do not show enthusiasm at all. Studies have shown that in many cases people refused to have Panchayats created to do developmental work. The finances of all local bodies particularly village Panchayats fell after 1920. For example, the Government noted that in 1923 all Village Panchayats in the state were in arrears of income. This situation continued in later years also. Infact, one of the reasons for the failure of the 1931 Elementary Education regulation was the financial malfunctioning of local bodies in the state.

Education Finances 1900-1921

The financing of Primary and Secondary education between 1900 and 1940, overall can be studied in two periods with the year 1921 when orders were issued on the Education Memorandum as cut off date.

Considering the twenty years between 1900 and 1920, as far as total expenditure on education as such is concerned in Mysore State the amount doubled by 1915 itself. It rose from Rs.1148276 in 1900 – 01 to Rs.2124860 in 1915 – 16. During the next five years it remarkably shot up to Rs.4165137. This jump is very significant when seen in the context of the fact that between 1900-01 and 1905-06, the increase was just little more that Rs.1 lakh and between 1905-06 and 1910 –11 it rose by over Rs.5 lakhs and between 1910-11 and 1915-16 it rose by a little more than Rs.3 lakhs.

Next we may take the amounts spent by Mysore Government during the period under consideration on several aspects of Primary and Secondary Education going by a reverse order from Secondary to Primary stage. The table indicates that there was no systematic attempt at regulating the spending. Because we see that there is no pattern in either increase or decrease in all the heads. Nor do we see any systematic or regular jump.

Next the several sources of income for this expenditure may be noted. The Reports classify the sources as shown below:-

State Funds
Local Rates/Cessess
Municipal Funds
Fees
Miscellaneous Sources

TABLE 35

Percentage of Expenditure on Service Heads

	1900-01	*1905-06*	*1910-11*	*1915-16*	*1920-21*
High School boys	9.19	11.13	8.81	7.62	7.3
High School girls	0.43	0.51	0.73	0.80	0.90
A.V.Schools boys (Middle)	11.95	11.48	9.76	9.57	10.02
A.V.Schools girls (Middle)	2.59	2.01	1.72	1.51	1.51
Vernacular Middle Schools boys	4.90	4.89	3.90	3.45	4.02
Vernacular Middle Schools girls	3.27	4.03	3.54	3.72	4.01
Primary Schools boys	19.14	16.64	16.27	15.80	17.20
Primary Schools girls	6.38	5.15	3.92	3.40	4.00

During the twenty year period under consideration State Funds were spent on all items of Primary and Secondary

Education (see Table) and naturally it accounted for a major share in the expenditure 40% to 70% of total expenditure on all aspects of education in the State. In this period Local Cesses and Municipal Funds, accounts for the rest.

Next the contribution of the several sources to the eight heads under Primary and Secondary Education may be considered. It is very interesting to note, that the State Funds were used for the development of Secondary, Middle and Primary School Education for both boys and girls. But significantly Local cessess and Rates were not used for High Schools at all. But Municipal Funds accounted for 10% to 15% of the amount spent from State funds for this head. Further in the case of Anglo- Vernacular Schools Local cesses and Municipal Funds accounted for 10% to 15% and some times a little more to what was spent from State Funds. But in the case of Vernacular Middle schools Local and Municipal funds accounted for as much as 90% to 95% of what was spent from State Funds. Lastly, regarding Primary Schools while Municipal Funds accounted for a very meagre amount of expenditure local cessess, accounted for 6 to 8 times more than the amounts spent from State Funds for these Schools.

1921 to 1941

Considering the total expenditure on education during the twenty years between 1921-1941, there was a remarkable jump from Rs. 4165137 in 1920 to Rs. 6073703 in 1925. Thereafter it rose to Rs. 6810292 in 1930; fell to Rs. 6380131 in 1935 and again sharply rose to Rs.7161085 in 1940.

The table below indicates the percentages of expenditure to total expenditure on Primary Middle and Secondary Schools during the period.

TABLE 36

Growth of Financial Allocation to Education

Heads	*1925*	*1930*	*1935*	*1940*
High Schools Boys	9.82	9.12	7.68	7.65
High Schools girls	1.02	0.86	0.95	1.37
Middle Schools boys	25.00	13.00	11.39	11.72
Middle Schools girls	—	1.99	1.99	2.23
Primary Schools boys	25.64	23.78	25.53	26.88
Primary Schools girls	6.20	5.38	6.39	6.41

As in the case of the earlier period there was no systematic attempt at spending and increases and falls in percentages, spent on the heads do not indicate any regular pattern.

Regarding the share of State Funds, Local Cessess and Municipal Funds for Secondary, Middle and Primary Education during the period under consideration it was similar to the trend between 1900 and 1920. Hence it does not call for specific comment.

7

Major Findings of the Study

1.1. Modern India's historiography is lopsided in several ways. While it is understandable that historical writings when the country was under colonial control did not focus on many important aspects the country's development, it is surprising that this situation continues in the post-Independence period also. The concentration has been on the political and economic aspects basically. Very important cultural aspects such as the development and impact of education continue to remain neglected areas of historical research. Secondly, and equally significantly the history and developments in the princely states described as native states, princely India or Indian India remain a neglected field by and large.

1.2 The princely states which were under indirect rule constitute an important chapter of colonial experience. The totality of colonial experience can be grasped only when the history of princely states is studied. For, as seen in the present study, colonial rule was similar both in British India and the states. This point has been effectively brought out by James Manor. British indirect rule was different to the extent that in the states, everything was managed as directed by the British masters by a native administration.

1.3 The historiography of Mysore which was considered by many as a progressive state is very meager. The authors who have published their studies have concentrated by and large on the political and economic aspects and have not touched on such an important subject as education especially at the primary and Secondary levels.

1.4 Mysore State in the closing years of the 19th century and through the 20th century was described as a Model State. This appellation was used both in the newspapers and public references to the state. But, there was no attempt at clearly stating the reasons why princely Mysore was described as Model State. Perhaps, the fact that there were two representatives bodies in the state, the fact that Mysore was ruled by benevolent and progressive minded maharaj as and very capable dewans; the fact that the state witnessed very significant economic and industrial development may among other things be taken as some of the justifications for Mysore being called model state.

1.5 But recent research on various aspects of the history of Mysore has questioned the correctness of the state being called Model State. Perhaps the first to attempt a study on this line was D.R. Gustafson. In his dissertation he observed that this praise was often the result of an exaggerated implication of certain measures adopted by the Mysore administration. Similarly, in her study of labour in Bangalore city, Janaki Nair has criticized the Model State description on the ground that the labour policies pursued by the state were not progressive at all.

1.6 A history of education in Modern India and especially in modern Mysore would go a long way in either proving or disproving atleast partially, the model state reputation. Again a study of education in Modern India or as in the present case, a princely state in Modern India is very significant because education implies, civilizing, modernizing, and creating a system of producing clerks to fill the bureaucracy.

2.1 The colonial power entered Mysore state after the IV Anglo – Mysore war. The basic objective placed before the new administration was the systematic collection of revenue so that the subsidy due to the East India company could be realized. Naturally the precolonial administration had to be swept away and the new system had to be the introduced. It is in this context that the 1813 debate in House of Commons and the 1822 Report regarding the education system that prevailed in Mysore has to be understood.

The 1813 debate in the House of Commons indicates the British intentions of introducing modern education in India because, in the view of the colonial power, the people of India needed religious and moral instruction.

This was their civilizing mission but they had to justify themselves and hence the Report giving them data about indigenous education which according to the Assistant College of Srirangapatna was only just sufficient for the ordinary transactions of daily life. This was not education obviously, according to them.

So what was education according to the colonial power? What was the aim and purpose of education in India while these questions were not immediately or directly answered in the context of Mysore, the schools started in Mysore between 1832 and 1856 by the Christian Missionaries make it clear that the civilizing mission was very strongly present.

2.2 Government entered into educational activity in Mysore after 1854 when the Woods Dispatch was applied to the state. The Devereux Scheme had nothing very significant except in proposing it and as it was brought into effect the purpose of introduction of education came out clearly. This will be referred to later on. But the available data for the period between 1859 and 1863 which is not very clear indicates that beginning from a total of 100 children in 1859 - 60 the number of school going children increased by 57%. But the figures of the base year indicate the poor response to education.

2.3 The next stage in the history of Primary and Secondary education in Mysore state was the Hobli School scheme. This was developed by B.L. Rice in the context of a remark by the Government of India that there were very few schools for female children and that there was need to increase the number of Vernacular schools in the state. According to this scheme there was to be one school in every hobli, where by no child would be more than 4 1/2 miles away from a school. In itself this was something terrible. To expect a child between 6 and 11 years of age to travel on an average 9 miles every day naturally, at a time when carts were the only means of popular and easily accessible means of transport, affordability was a big issue. Only those who could afford to send children to school by cart would do so.

2.4 Rice had fondly hoped that once this scheme became operative quickly 50000 children would attend school. His hope or dream was never realized. Even in 1880 that is to say 10 years after the scheme came into operation only 16502 children were attending schools.

2.5 It is very interesting that a majority of these children were this goes to prove in unmistakable terms that when modern education was introduced in a big way the Hindus were the first to take to it. Further, though clear data is not available most of the children were Brahmins. Thus the bait of government employment on passing out of a Hobli school was taken only by Hindus and among them by Brahmins and Muslims and Panchamas were far away in the race for government jobs.

2.6 Going by district wise figures of the number of hobli schools Mysore took the first place, followed by Bangalore, Kolar, Shimoga, Tumkur, Chitradruga, Hassan and kadur.

2.7 Taking the total member of Hobli Schools between 1868 and 1900 it increased from 143 schools for a district in 1868 to 637 schools in 1880. That is, the total increase was 493 schools for 10 years or an average of 49 schools every year or 6 schools in a district on an average. Similarly the total number of schools increased from 636 in 1880 to 1376 in 1900 that is 20 years after. This means, some 740 school were started over the period of 20 years otherwise. Some 37 schools were started on an average in a year or 4 schools on average in a district every year. The fall in averages could be taken as indicating regression in the Hobli School Scheme as such.

2.8 The growth of schools in the Hobli Schools Scheme was not uniform or even, rather it was lopsided.

2.9 Since schools were to be started only on application from the people in the concerned areas every by 1900 we see that only 1376 villages wanted schools for their children.

2.10 Female education is a very interesting and important subjects. But it a complex field which has to be discussed separately. However to give completeness to the picture, some references have been made here.

2.11 Schools for female children were considered as "exotic" institutions and they faced several problems Non availability of female teachers was one of the most significant of these. The other important problem was fear of conversion to Christianity.

2.12 Even as late as in the 1920 there were very few people in the state who whole heartedly favoured educating their female children in the modern primary and secondary schools. This was very natural because if girls were to be educated they had to be for its own sake. Perhaps none even remotely thought of girls coming out schools being employed as clerks in the administration.

2.13 The available data reveals that quite a few of the girls who went to schools were Brahmins and came from affluent families. Thus education of girls for its own sake was something prevalent only in affluent Brahmins families and perhaps to a small extent in other communities.

2.14 However taking the figures for the development of government and aided primary schools for girls we see some interesting details. While in 1869 - 70 were 5 government girls schools with some 27 pupils on an average it rose to 11 schools nearly a decade later with 42 children on an average. The aided schools were much more popular. There were 28 schools in this class in 1869 - 70 educating 69 girl children on an average. It rose up to 39 schools in 1878 with 75 girl children on an average.

2.15 M. Visveswaraya who was an idealist and a follower of Gokhale introduced the Compulsory Elementary Education law in Mysore in 1913. The law had many loop - holes to which references will be made later.

Four years after it was introduced the Government was optimistic. But within the next 3 years the scheme went on the rocks. It failed miserably. The large number of warning notices issued in 1916, 1917, 1918, 1919 indicate how it was gradually failing. Convictions could not be sustained under this law. Further looking at the general trend particularly in the context of Report of 1919 - 20 one gets the feeling the Government was suppressing the actual figures relating to failure of this law.

2.18 The Development of Primary schools after 1921 does not call of or any specific comment. More schools were started and more children went to schools. But other developments were taking place.

2.19 The 1931 law is an important landmark in the history of primary education. That year it was handed over the local self governing bodies in the state.

2.20 Local bodies in the state were not effective because of financial problems and the very ambitious move of 1931 was bound to fail. Yet another reason was the lack of interest on the part of the local public men to work on the local bodies and on LEA's and manage schools. After 1931 Primary Education in Mysore State declined.

2.21. During the late 1830s and later the Government noticed that there was wastage and retardation in Primary Education. This phenomenon was not new only for this period. But it was new in so far as Government was nothing it. All the children in the Primary Schools did not complete the course.

The dropping out was very heavy. In 1927 - 28 of a assumed, 100 in the Primary schools, in Mysore, 46.1 were in the I year while the remaining 54% approximately were distributed between 3 classes following. Similarly in 1931 -

32, 52.42 of children of a assumed 100 were in the I year while, the remaining 48% approximately were distributed between the next 3 classes following. While Government diagnised several reasons for this, it did not stress as it should have, the fact that education at the Primary level was not yet popular at the mass level in Mysore.

3.1 Middle school education was in some ways worse then the Primary Education. This was because at the termination of this stage a person could seek Government employment after reaching the minimum entry age. The attraction was that English was taught in some of these schools. In fact in 1876, Government announced that only those who had passed the Middle Schools Examination could enter state services in the salary of Rs.20/ - per month.

3.2 Till 1921 as a natural consequence very few children took to this stage of education. As in the case of primary education development was not even and in some district such as Bangalore and Mysore there were several Middle Schools and while in the others it was very poor development.

3.3 Government diagnised reasons as non availability of good English teachers. But another fact was, for a long time Government jobs were not popular.

3.4 Retardation was remarkable. In 1873 - 74 out of a total of 104, children in the Middle Schools only 7 were in the 4th year. Working out the percentage is useless. The figures speak for themselves.

3.5 Even more than the Primary and Middle stages High school education was tied up to the Government jobs. But as in the case of Middle Schools there was a High School Scheme after which one could take to teaching profession in the schools.

3.6 As in the case of the two earlier stages High school was also a stage to which girls were not sent in a big way till the 1830s The number of girls, in High schools even in 1915 - 16 was about 1/3 the number of boys.

3.7 Castewise figures are more interesting, in 1910 while there were 3146 Brahmin children there were no non - Brahmin children. Two years later there was a spurt with 1351 non Brahmin Hindu children as against 3607 Brahmin children. This was evidently due to the non - Brahmin movement and the Demand of the backward classes for education with English so that they could seek Government jobs.

4.1 While the British did not consider indigenous schools as useful they did not carefully consider whether the system they introduced would suit the needs of the local people.

4.2 Quite apart from all the high phrases in the woods Despatch, the education system they introduced in India and Mysore was clearly meant to fulfil the needs of the bureaucracy. This is clear in the Devereux Scheme and the Hobli School Scheme.

4.3 The British in Mysore favoured vernacular education but the administration needed men with English knowledge. This contradiction cannot be explained at all.

4.4 Visveswaraya was an idealist and a person who attempted to formulate scheme for the all round development of Mysore. He considered education to be the only remedy for the ills of the nation. But would the education then being suit the people? He thought so.

The 1913 law for Compulsory Primary Education had loopholes and it proved quickly to be ineffective.

It also proved that Education could not be imposed by Government.

4.5 The Backward Class Movement was basically aimed at securing more jobs for the backward classes in state services and more educational facilities for them. It is a fact that till 1830s Panchamas were in many cases prevented from entering schools with pupils of other castes. But it is also clear that non - Brahmin Hindu children did not take to education for other reasons also.

4.6 A community, whose literacy in English was less than 5% in 1911 was considered backward. Hence backward class movement with its demand for Government jobs and the recommendation of the Miller Committee regarding education and jobs was tied up with Primary and especially High school education. But the available data presented by Lelah Dushkin has shown that as late as in 1930 even there were very few backward class persons in Government jobs.

4.7 Education memorandum of 1921 was an ambitious scheme and it could not be fully implemented in the state.

4.8 The 1930 law on Elementary Education was also ambitious. But this law also failed. Rather it resulted in a clear retardation of Primary Education. Financial reasons and lack of initiative at local level account for this.

5.1 The Department of Public Instruction started in 1857 made education a state enterprise. It started as a small group of officials and over the years grew.

5.2 School inspection was faced by problems such as distance to be traveled, bureaucratic responsibilities of official etc. Naturally as noted by the Government inspection was not followed up.

5.3 Over the years the face of inspection underwent remarkable change. Earlier it was a department which had to look into all problems faced by people and later it became more bureaucratic and technical. This could not be avoided.

5.4 Hobli School Panchayats though ambitiously constituted did not do much work except an overall supervision. So were the Village Schools, Committees. The visits of revenue officers were of similar nature, because Revenue Officials had the work of their own department and this was an unwanted additional burden.

5.5 The MRA and Legislature Council though enthusiastic did not have the necessary powers to check the Government till 1924. Afterwards they did forcefully criticize the administration but it would take time, before these bodies would become effective.

5.6 Even as the 1931 statute failed the School Boards also failed, generally. Meetings were irregular and the number of subjects discussed was very large for any meaningful debate to have taken place.

6.1 Unlike in Pre - modern periods modern education is a charge on the state expenditure.

6.2 Until 1854, the Mysore state authorities did not spend any thing on education at all. Missionary institutions financed their schools and the ruler financed the Rajahs School.

6.3 Data regarding expenditure on Primary and Secondary education which is composite with other heads indicates that it was meagre. But there was a steady increase from Rs.9013 in 1854 to Rs.35340 in 1857 and to Rs.214407 in 1880.

6.4 Local funds accounted for a major share in the educational expenditure in Mysore State from the beginning. But during the 1830s and later since, local bodies were malfunctioning, finances were in problems and this affected education. But the results are not clear.

6.5 Between 1900 and 1940 when the study closes there was no systematic attempt at spending on Primary and Secondary schools.

6.6 During this period state funds accounted for 40% to 70% of total educational expenditure.

6.7 State funds were used for all heads of Primary and Secondary education.

6.8 Local and Municipal funds were not used for High schools at all.

6.9 In the case of Vernacular Middle Schools Local and Municipal funds almost matched State Funds.

6.10 In the case of Primary Schools it may without exaggeration be observed that Local Funds met the expenditure up to 8 times more than state expenditure.

6.11 Regarding total expenditure, Primary Education took away between 15% to 26% of total expenses. The rest of the amount was shared unevenly between other heads.

6.12 The state did not accord priority to female educational expenses at all. It never rose beyond 6.40% of total expenditure. Middle schools of the vernacular type and middle schools for girls were even worse.

A general observation may be made regarding the Model State Praise for Mysore. While superficially it seems Mysore was a Model State from the point of the big industries, the representative bodies, and the benevolent rulers and their

Dewans, when considered from the point of education at the Primary and Secondary levels one gets serious doubts. Whether Mysore was a Model state at all. Several of the schemes failed and mostly education at these levels was not popular at the mass level. Womens education was in very bad shape.

The British delegitimised the native indigenous education system. They replace this with another oriented towards making clerks for the administration. But for long the bait of Government jobs was not taken by many people and certainly not the masses. Later this bait led to the cleavage between caste groups. Finally women were neglected in the educational sense also.

Bibliography

PRIMARY SOURCES

Karnataka State Archives

General & Revenue Secretariat of the Government of His Highness the Maharaja of Mysore, General Miscellaneous, file collection, 1840-1940.

General and Revenue Secretariat of the Government of His Highness the Maharaja of Mysore Reforms, file Collection, 1924.

General and Revenue Secretariat of the Government of His Highness, the Maharaja of Mysore, Legislation, file collection, 1912-1940.

General and Revenue Secretariat of the Government of His Highness the Maharaja of Mysore Education file collection, 1853-1940.

Mysore Annual Administrative Reports, 1856-1940.

Monthly Proceedings of the Government of His Highness the Maharaja of Mysore 1856-1940.

Proceedings of the Mysore Representative Assembly 1881-1940.

Proceedings of the Mysore Legislative Council 1924-1940.

Reports of the Department of Public Instruction in Mysore 1865-1940.

Proceedings of the Mysore Economic Conference 1916-1921.

Mysore Code Vol. II & IX

Review of the Progress of Education in the Mysore State during the period 1916-17 to 1921-22, Bangalore Government Press, 1927.

Progress of Education in Mysore State 1930-1944, Bangalore, Government Press, 1946.

Review of the Progress of Education in Mysore State, for the Quniquinnium 1911 to 1916, Bangalore, Government Press, 1916.

Review of the Progress of Education in Mysore State, for the December 1922-23 to 1931-32, Bangalore, Government Press, 1935.

Education Manual, Parts 1, 2, 3, 1918.

Manual of Important Orders Series, S Education, 1918.

Selections from the Old Records of the Mysore Government Secretariat. Mysore Gazette, 1900-1940.

Education in Mysore (C.R. Reddy) 949.

Report of the Education Committee 1917-18.

Report of the Committee Appointed to consider necessary steps for the Adequate Representation of the Communities in the Services (1918).

Proceedings of Mysore Economic Conference 1911-1916.

Opinions Regarding the starting of the Mysore Economic Conference 1911.

Mysore Blue Book and Publicity Journal.

National Archives of India

Selection from Educational Records of the Government of India, Vol. I Educational Reports 1859-71 (New Delhi: National Archives, 1960).

Richey F.A., (Ed), Selection from Educational Records Part II, 1840-1859 (Calcutta: Government Printing Press, 1922).

Sharp, H; selections from Educational Records, Part I, 1781-1839, (Calcutta: Government Printing Press, 1920).

United Theological College, Bangalore.

The Bangalore Missionary Conference Collection (BOX 5).

The Church of South India Collection, KCD Materials.

The London Missionary Society collection (BOX 53).

Various Private Papers.

BOOKS

Anil Seal: *The Emergence of Indian Nationalism*, (Cambridge; at the University Press, 1968).

Arthur Mathew: *The Education of India 1835-1920*, (London; Faber and Gwyer, Second Ed; MeMXXVII).

Baker C.J., and Washbrook, D.A., *South India Political Institutions and Political Change 1880-1940*, (Delhi; The Macmillan Co. of India Ltd, 1975).

Banerji A., *Speeches by Sir Albion Banerji* (1916-26) (Bangalore 1926).

Basu, Aparna, *The Growth of Education and Political Development in India 1998-1920* (New Delhi; Oxford University Press, 1974).

Basu, A.N., *Indian Education in Parliamentary Papers*, part I (Bombay; Asia Publishing House, 1974).

Basu, B.D; *History of Education in India under the Rule of the East India Company* (Calcutta, the Modern Review Office).

Bilgrami, Syed Amir Ali, *English Education in India* (Madras; Lawrance Asylim Steam Press, 1902).

The British Administration of Mysore, (London; by a native of Mysore, 1976).

Chandrashekara, N.S., *Dewan Seshadri Iyer* (New Delhi; Publications Division, 1981).

Chandrashekara, N.S., *Dewan Rangacharlu* (New Delhi; Publication Division, 1968).

Chandrashekar S., *Dimensions of Sociopolitical Changes in Mysore 1918-1941.* (New Delhi; Ashish Publishing House, 1985).

Chaudary, V.C.P., *Imperial Policy of British in India 1876-1880 Birth of Indian Nationalism,* (Calcutta, Punthi Pustak, 1968).

Datta K.K., *Social History of Modern India,* (Delhi; The Macmillan Co., P., Ltd, 1975).

Desai, A.R., *Social Background of India Nationalism* (Bombay: Popular Prakshan, Fourth Ed, 1966).

Devegowda, A.C., and Parameshwaran, T.R., *History of Education in Mysore* (Bangalore; Department of Education and Youth Service, 1985).

Dharmpal; *The Beautiful Tree* (New Delhi; Impex Biblia, 1983). *Experience: Educational Reformation in India* (Calcutta; J.C. Basak Beadon Street).

Fleming, Danial Johnson; *Schools with a Message in India,* (London; Humphy Milford, Oxford University Press, 1921).

Forbers R., *India of the Princes,* (London; 1939).

Fraber, A.J., *Village Education in India,* (London; Oxford University Press, 1920).

Gopal, S., *British Policy in India 1858-1905,* (Cambridge University Press, 1911).

Gokhale, G.K., *The Elementary Education Bill* (Poona; Arya Bhusan Press, 1911).

Hettne, B., *The Political Economy of Indirect Rule Mysore; 1881, 1947,* (New Delhi; Ambika Publications, 1978).

Hortog, P., *Some Aspects of Indian Education Past and Present,* (London, Oxford University Press, 1929).

Heimsat, Charles, H., *Indian Nationalism and Hindu Social Reforms,* (Bombay; Oxford University Press, 1964).

Ismail, M., *My Public Life,* (London; 1954).

Ismail, M., *Speeches by Sir Mirza M. Ismail,* Vol. (1926-30) Vol. II (1931-36) Vol. III (1936-38) and Vol. IV (1939-41) (Bangalore, 1930-1942).

James, H.R., *Education and Statesmanship in India (1797-1910),* (London; Longans Green and Co., 1911).

Joshi, K.L.; and Shukla P.D., (Ed), *Women and Education in India,* in women and education (Paris; UNESCO, 1953).

Kamat, S.U., *Karnataka State Gazetteer,* Vol. I (Bangalore; Government of Karnataka, 1983).

Krishna Kumar; *Political Agenda of Education,* (New Delhi; Sage Publications, 1991).

Lajpat Rai, Lala; *The Problems of National Education in India* (London; George Allen and Unwin Ltd, 1920).

Magnus, Sir, Philip; *Educational Aims and Efforts 1880-1910* (London; Longmans Green and Co., 1910).

Mahmood, Syed; *History of English Education in India 1791-1893,* (Aligarh; Honorary Secretary of the M.A.O. College, 1895).

Majumdar, Bhagaban Prasad; *First Fruits of English Education 1817-1957,* (Calcutta; Bookland P. Ltd; 1973).

Majumdar, R.C., (Ed) *British Paramountacy and Indian Renaissance,* Part 2, (Bombay; Bharatiya Vidya Bhavan, 1965).

Manor J., *Political Changes in an Indian State—Mysore 1917-1956,* (New Delhi; Manohar Publications, 1977).

Mathur, Y.B., *Women's Education in India* (Bombay; Oxford University Press, 1973).

Mcuuly, Bruee Tiebout; *English Education and the Origins of Indian Nationalism* (Glomester, Mass, Petersmith, 1966).

Meston, W., *Indian Education Policy* (Madras Christian Literature Society, 1936).

Mirza Ismail; *Views and Opinions on his Retirement from the office of the Dewan of Mysore,* (Bangalore; 1942).

Moore, R.J., *Sir Charles Wood's Indian Policy 1853-1866.* (Manchester, 1966).

Mysore Representative Assembly (a presentation) (Bangalore; 1903).

Nanda, B.R., *Gokhale, the Indian Moderates the British Raj.* (New Delhi; Oxford University, Press, 1979).

Natarajan, S., *A Country of Social Reform in India,* (Bombay, Asia Publishing House, 1959).

Nurulia, Syed and Naik, J.P., *History of Education in India,* (Bombay; Macmillan and Co. Ltd, 1943).

Paranjpe, M.R., *A Sources Book of Modern Indian Education,* (Bombay, Macmillan, Co., 1938).

Rao, K.S., *Sir Mirza M. Ismail: Architect of Modern Mysore.* (Mysore; 1941).

Rao, M.S., *Modern Mysore,* Vol. I-II (Bangalore; 1936).

Rao, M.S., *Ten Years of Native Rule in Mysore* (Madras; 1891).

Rao, V.S.N., *Mokshagundam Visveswaraya: His Life and Work.* (Mysore; 1973).

Roy Choudhury, S.S., "The Educational Pattern in Pre-British India," *Modern Review,* Aug 1953.

Sastri K.N.V., *The Administration of Mysore under Sir Mark Cubbon* (London; 1932).

Samiullh Beg; Mirza Yar. Jung; *Educational Problems of India,* (Secunderabad; B.V.R. Balreddy and Co.; 1925).

Satthianandhan, S., *History of Education in the Madras Presidency,* (Madras; Srinivasa Varadachari and Co., 1894).

Sequeira, T.N., *The Education of India,* (Bombay; 1939).

Subba Rao, N., *Hindu Social Progress,* Indian Progress.

Series No.1 (Madras; G.A. Natesan and Co., 1904).

Sumit Sarkar; *Bibliography of Social Reform Movements in the Eighteenth and Nineteenth Century* (Now Delhi; Indian Council for Historical Research, 1975).

Urs, M.K., *Address of Sir M.Kantharaj Urs (Dewan of Mysore 1919-1922) to the Representative Assembly* Vol. II (Mysore; 1953).

Vaikuntham, Y., *Education and Social Change in South India, 1880-1920,* (Madras; New Era Publications, 1982).

Viveswaraya, M., *District Development Scheme Economic Progress by Forced,* (Marches, Bangalore; 1940).

Visveswaraya, M., *Memoirs of My Working Life.* (Bombay; 1951).

Visveswaraya, M., *Planned Economy for India* (Bangalore; 1936).

Visveswaraya, M., *Speeches by Sir M.Visveswaraya* 1910-11 to 1916-17 (Bangalore;1917).

Wadiyar, K., *Speeches by His Highness Maharaja Sri Krishnaraja Wadiyar Bahadur, Maharaja of Mysore 1902-1933.* (Mysore; 1934).

ARTICLES

Ramakrishnan, R; "Education and Social Progress; The Politics of Backward Classes in Princely Mysore 1921-1941", *Quarterly Journal of Mythic Society,* Vol. 73, No. 3 1982

Gayathri Devi A.H., "M Visveswarayas Village Improvement Scheme", *Quarterly Journal of Mythic Society,* Vol. 75, 1984.

UNPUBLISHED DISSERTATIONS

Gayathri Devi A.H., *The Development of Local Self Government in Prineely Mysore* (Bangalore University, 1990).

Visveswaraya, M., *Speeches by Sir M.Visveswaraya 1910-11 to 1916-17* (Bangalore; 1917).

Wadiyar. K., *Speeches by His Highness Maharaja Sri Krishnaraja Wadiyar Bahadur, Maharaja of Mysore 1902-1933.* (Mysore; 1934)

ARTICLES

Ramakrishnan, R., "*Education and Social Progress; The Politics of Backward Classes in Princely Mysore 1921-1941.*"

Quarterly Journal of Mythic Society, Vol. 73, No.3, 1982.

Gayathri Devi A.H., "M. Visveswaraya's Village Improvement Scheme", *Quarterly Journal of Mythic Society*, Vol. 75, 1984.

UNPUBLISHED DISSERTATION

Gayathri Devi A.H., *The Development of Local Self Government in Princely Mysore* (Bangalore University, 1990).

Gustafson D.R. *Myosre; 1881-1902:* The Making of a Model State (University of Wisconsin, 1969).

Lelah Dushkin, *The Non-Brahmin Movement in Princely Mysore* (Pennsylvannia University, 1974).

Rama Krishnan, R., *The Role of the Press in Princely Mysore 1859-1947* (Bangalore University 1987).

Sargur Doss, M., *Educational Policy in Madras Presidency 1880-1900*, (Madras University, Madras, 1961).

Vihal Rao, Y, *Education and Learning in Andhra under the East India Company*, (Karnataka University, Dharwar, 1967).

Index

A

Administrative System of Mysore, 8

Anglo-Mysore War, 99

Anglo-Vernacular Schools, 34, 35, 39, 42, 50, 95

B

Backward Classes Movement, 56, 106

Backward Communities, 58

Bangalore-Kadur, 101

BN Seal Committee, 10

Brahmin Community, 22

British
- Administration, 90
- Colonial Penetration, 4
- Colonialism, 3
- India, 1, 7, 97
- Labor, 47
- Paramountcy, 45
- Policy and Mysore, 6
- Rule, 1, 9, 45

C

Christian Missionaries, 9, 12, 13, 90, 99
- Organization, 4

Colonialism, 3, 4

Compulsory Education, 25, 26, 28
- Scheme, 59

Compulsory Elementary Education, 10, 54, 102, 105
- Regulations, 88

Compulsory Primary Education, 24

D

Depressed Classes, 28

Development of Education
- in India, 7
- in Mysore, 7

Devereux Scheme, 49, 50, 100

District Boards, 88

Doctrine of Lapse, 1

E

East India Company, 8, 45, 46, 90, 99

Economic Development, 3

Education, 3-5, 8, 11, 12, 13, 14, 26
- Expenditure of-, 91
- Financing of-, 90, 93
- System, 99

Educational
- Census, 28
- Development, 4
- Institutions, 76
- Policy, 5
- System, 4, 6, 49

Elementary Education, 54, 55

Elementary Education Act, 4, 30

Elementary Education in Mysore, 72
England, 7, 46
English East India Company, 1, 8, 45
English Education Act, 1870, 54
English Education, 7
English Language, 48, 72

F

Female Education, 19, 32
Fourth Mysore War, 8

G

Gokhale, Gopalkrishna, 54, 102
Gokhale's Bill, 55
Govt. Girls Schools Details, 19-22

H

Halifax Despatch, 4, 46
Hassa, 14, 25
Higher Secondary Education, 42
Hobli School, 17, 19, 23
  Details, 16
  Panchayats, 73, 107
  Scheme, 15, 19, 22, 23, 24, 50, 79, 100, 101, 105

I

Imperial Legislature Council, 54
Indian History Congress, 2
Instrument of Transfer, 9, 51
Irish Education Act, 1892, 54
Iyer, Seshadri, 52, 56, 81

K

Kolar Gold Fields, 30

L

Liberal Education, 48
Local Cesses, 95
Local Education Authorities, 73, 87, 103
Local Functions, 73-75
Local Fund Rules, 72
Local Funds Boards, 91, 92
London Christian Mission, 12
London Mission, 12

M

Madras University, 44
Middle School Education, 5
Miller Committee, 10, 56-59, 106
Modern Education System, 76
Monford Committee, 73
Municipal Funds, 94, 95, 108
Munro, Thomas, 11
Muslim Education, 6
Mysore
  Economic Conference, 10, 54, 71
  Elementary Education Regulation, 1930, 5, 72, 73
  Legislature Assembly, 10
  Legislature Council, 88
  Representative Assembly, 9, 52, 53, 73, 77, 81, 87, 88, 107
  Role of-, 87
Mysore Treaty, 10
Mysore University, 54

N

Nagar and Shimoga Provinces, 8
Nagar Revolt, 90

P

Panchama Caste Group, 17
Paramount Power, 6, 10
Peasant Uprising, 8

Praja Mitra Mandal, 56
Primary and Secondary Education, 91, 93-95, 100, 107, 108, 109
Primary Education, 5, 6, 11, 22, 24, 30, 54, 58, 71, 88, 103, 104, 108
Primary School System, 34
Princely India, 97
Princely States, 1, 2, 10, 97
Public Instructions, D/O, 77, 83, 86, 106
    Reorganization, 83, 86

R

Rao, Hayavadana, 2, 3
Rao, M Sharma, 2, 3
Rice, BL, 50, 51, 100

S

School Boards, 87
School Education, 11
Secondary Education, 54
Secondary Education System, 34
Shimoga, 14, 25
Society, 33
State Funds, 95
Subsidiary Treaty, 1799, 8, 45, 90

T

Tippu Sultan, 8
Tumkur, 14
Types of Schools, 34

U

USA, 53

V

Vernacular Schools, 34, 35, 37, 39, 42, 50, 95
Village Panchayats, 92
Village School Committee, 81, 82
Village School Fund, 72
Visveswaraya, M, 5, 10, 52, 53, 54, 56, 102, 105

W

Wesleyan Mission, 12
Western Culture, 9
Wodeyar, Chamarajendra X, 9
Wodeyar, Krishna Raja III, 8, 12, 45
Wodeyar, Krishna Raja, 8, 9
Women's Education, 6
Woods Dispatch, 49, 99

□□□